CAPE COD COLLECTED

A Selection of the Cape's Greatest Stories

Cover Painting
"Highland Light"

by Kathryn Kleekamp
www.SandwichArt.com
See page 143 for more info.

CAPE COD COLLECTED

A Selection of the Cape's Greatest Stories

Jim Coogan
Jack Sheedy

Harvest Home Books
East Dennis, Massachusetts
www.harvesthomebooks.info

CAPE COD COLLECTED

First Printing – April 2015
Second Printing – May 2019
Third Printing – March 2022

Published by
Harvest Home Books
P. O. Box 1181, East Dennis, Massachusetts 02641

ISBN 978-0-989307-34-5

Cover design and text layout by Kristen vonHentschel

Printed in the United States of America

Additional copies of **Cape Cod Collected** and the authors' previous
Cape Cod books may be obtained by contacting Harvest Home Books
or by visiting www.harvesthomebooks.info.

Cape Odd
Cape Cod Harvest
(Coogan & Sheedy)

Sail Away Ladies
Cecelia the Seal Gets a Meal
Clarence the Cranberry Who Couldn't Bounce
Priscilla the Amazing Pinkywink
Sears Point
Tommy Tent-boy's Turkey
(Coogan)

Dennis Journal
(Sheedy)

Visit us at www.harvesthomebooks.info

TABLE OF CONTENTS

Table of Contents Continued...

FOREWORD

Cape Cod Collected began in the usual way, the two of us seated around a table at our "office" in a local coffee shop with cups of coffee, a cruller or two, some papers scattered about, and with ideas bouncing back and forth as if participating in a leisurely ping pong match. Caffeine and a common interest in local history, combined with hours of compiling, editing, and proofreading, have produced the book you now hold in your hands. It is our fifth collaborative effort – our previous titles being *Cape Cod Companion* (1999), *Cape Cod Voyage* (2001), *Cape Cod Harvest* (2007), and *Cape Odd* (2010) – which makes us one of Cape Cod's most prolific book writing teams. Yet, along with this achievement comes a great respect and admiration for the history we write about. We could never have published five books together without having such wonderful subject matter to share with our readers.

The tales presented in this collection represent some of our favorite Cape Cod stories, a recounting of past events that we've written about over the years, edited and packaged in such a way as to make them more accessible to our 21st century readers. In a sense, it is our "Greatest Hits" collection, as we feel these stories deserve another look from a new perspective. After all, Cape Cod is truly a place like no other.

Created out of a glacial age just 10,000 years ago – a blink of an eye in the geologic clock – Cape Cod has been the home to Native Americans, Mayflower Pilgrims, and a steady stream of Old Comers during the 17th and 18th centuries, as well as lots of interesting "New Comers" in more recent times. Over the centuries, generations of Cape Codders carved an existence from these sandy shores, earning their living both on the land and on the sea. With the sea came shipwrecks and Cape waters served as the final resting place for some 3,000 vessels and hundreds of lost mariners. Eighteen lighthouses and thirteen lifesaving stations were erected to aid them as they journeyed along the treacherous coastline.

When the flame of freedom was first lit, Cape Codders helped to fan those flames into an American Revolution. They took up arms during the War of 1812, the Civil War, and again during the First World War when a German U-boat surfaced off the coast and marked Orleans as the only attack against US soil during that conflict. More recent military campaigns have found Cape people no less involved.

And Cape Cod wouldn't be Cape Cod without its mysterious side and its dark secrets, from overlooked locations and interesting happenings to curious and intriguing tales featuring witches and pirates – even a vengeful playwright.

As we mentioned in our first book together, Cape Cod is a composite of thousands of stories which, in their aggregate, chronicle her interesting past. In this latest volume we have collected a smattering of some of our favorite stories to help paint the portrait of this truly historic place.

Jim Coogan & Jack Sheedy
East Dennis, MA
April 2015

Chapter 1

Early Days

Geologically speaking, Cape Cod is perhaps the newest part of the "New World," formed only ten or so millennia ago during a glacial epoch. First discovered by Native Americans around five thousand years ago, it was perhaps rediscovered by Vikings one thousand years ago according to Norse sagas. Unable to establish a permanent settlement, the Norse departed the New World, providing the Natives with a bit of a reprieve until European settlers arrived four centuries ago. And it has been an adventure ever since.

How Cape Cod Was Formed

Present day Cape Cod is not like the mainland to which it is attached. While the rocks of New England were formed millions of years ago, the Cape is relatively young and a product of wind, water, and glacial action. There are no outcroppings of solid rock here as can be found in other parts of the Northeast. The bedrock of granite lies far beneath the clay, silt, and sand that is part of our contemporary landscape.

Perhaps some fifty to seventy-five thousand years ago, a great sheet of ice formed over Greenland and Labrador. The cold period that produced mammoth glaciers lasted for hundreds, perhaps thousands of years. As the earth went into an extended deep freeze, the sea levels were lowered as water evaporated and fell as snow in the higher latitudes. Over time, the glacier moved slowly south acting like a giant bulldozer, gouging and scraping great valleys and pushing tons of material before it. At one point, it is estimated that almost one-third of the Northern Hemisphere was encased in ice.

When the first great wave of ice reached this area, some twenty to twenty-five thousand years ago, the terminal moraine, or final ridge of debris, was deposited in the present locations of Martha's Vineyard and Nantucket.

A second renewal of a southern ice sheet, which arrived around ten thousand years ago, stopped in the vicinity of the northern edge of what is now Cape Cod. In both eras, the melting ice created outwash channels that moved both water and till to the south, creating ancient rivers whose forgotten channels can be found today by soundings in Nantucket Sound and to the south of both Martha's Vineyard and Nantucket.

As the earth warmed, the ice melted and retreated northward. As sea levels rose, wave action began to shape the soft edges of the exposed land. The glacial debris was ground into sand, which then migrated and collected along the coast. Most of Provincetown, Barnstable's Sandy Neck, Nauset Spit, and all of Monomoy Island are perhaps the best examples of sand migration deposited by this wave action. On the ground that remained above sea level, the old outwash channels became the familiar rivers that are part of the present landscape. It is interesting to note that most all of these rivers, like their ancient predecessors, flow in a southerly direction.

Another shaping factor that occurred with the retreat of the glacier was the creation of Cape Cod's ponds and lakes. There are more than three hundred and fifty of them. Huge singular blocks of ice that had been part of the ice mass broke off and eventually melted, forming most of the bodies of fresh water that are common on Cape Cod. On the southern plains of both Cape Cod and the Islands, spring fed "kettle ponds" filled in the depressions left from of these large glacial ice chunks. In what would appear a confirmation of geologic theory, the largest boulders found on both the Cape and Islands are located on the northern edges of these land masses. Along the Cape's moraine are the rough highlands, rising up to about two hundred feet above sea level. The land in Barnstable village, for example, is much higher and rockier than is the ground at Hyannis, Cotuit, and Centerville. Geological borings confirm that the lighter materials under the surface of the land are situated on the southern slope of Cape Cod, Nantucket,

This 14-foot high boulder, known as Hokum Rock, was pushed here by a glacier and deposited in Dennis. Legend says it is named for a Native who lived nearby. Photo: Jack Sheedy

and Martha's Vineyard and are closer to sea level. The effect of this geology meant that farming tended to be a bit easier on the southern edges of the Cape and the Islands because the land was more level with fewer obstructions to plowing. A close look at Cape Cod villages on the south side will also reveal fewer stone walls.

The lasting impact of the great ice age can be visibly tracked today in the line of water towers that parallel the upland ridge along the Mid-Cape highway. These high points sit on the greatest extent of the debris field that was deposited eons ago. The constant winds that blow across the peninsula, coupled with the incessant wave action along the coastline, put the finishing touches on Cape Cod. But Cape Cod and the Islands are still a work in progress as far as the natural forces of wind and water are concerned. Each winter we see more and more erosion claiming exposed beach areas. Given enough time, the peninsula and its island cousins will eventually succumb to these forces. When that happens the geologic cycle will have come full circle.

The Realm of the Great Spirit

Geologists may claim that a half-mile high glacier of ice formed the peninsula of Cape Cod, but the Natives of the area had a much different and more colorful explanation of how the landmass was formed. They believed that the Great Spirit Kehtean created the lands and the waters that we see today as well as the skies that stretch overhead, thus providing a paradise teeming with bountiful rewards.

In addition, they believed that a local giant named Maushop created the islands of Nantucket and Martha's Vineyard with sands he emptied from his enormous moccasins. So large was Maushop that when he slept his frame stretched from Provincetown, where his head rested upon a pillow of sand dunes, to Falmouth, where his restless feet etched the jagged coastline. While he slept, he tossed and turned, his movements hollowing the land to produce ponds, valleys, and hills. In the town of Dennis, during one such nap, Maushop created Scargo Lake below and Scargo Hill above, as well as the pine trees encircling the lake and dotting the hill which sprouted from the ashes of his pipe. Smoke from his pipe formed thunderclouds that produced days of rain – enough rain, in fact, to fill the lake. Geologists, of course, have their own explanation involving a receding glacier and a large cake of melting ice that formed a water-filled hollow in the sandy terrain. Incidentally, the giant is also credited with creating the fog so prevalent in the area with smoke from his pipe, to the woe of seafarers over the centuries.

Maushop had five giant sons, whom he relied on to do all types of odd jobs as he slept, yet the local Pukwudgees, a band of rather impish little creatures with devious intent, were jealous of the snoozing giant and set upon the sons, killing them with their magical powers. The five were buried in the waters off Woods Hole, their graves covered with sand to produce what we today call the Elizabeth Islands. Again, geologists point to their glacier theory.

Another being who was important in the Native traditions, and who played a role in their daily lives, was Granny Squannit, or Tooquah-misquannit in the Native tongue. It is said she lived in a dune cave in the vicinity of the great marshes along the northern coastline of the Cape. She possessed singular physical features – she was short in stature with webbed fingers and long hair that concealed her face. One of her feet was larger than the other, thus creating strange footprints in the sands along the beaches. Yet her most distinguishing feature was a single eye in the very center of her forehead. She used herbs to concoct secret magic potions and was thus able to communicate with animals. Despite her talents and magic, she was envious of Maushop's special powers and once bargained with a whale to steal the giant's pipe, promising one thousand trout in payment. The whale had different ideas, though, and stole the pipe for himself. But that didn't stop Granny Squannit. She tricked the leviathan, luring it close to shore and when he was close enough she caused the tide to go out, beaching the whale. Perhaps she has something to do with the occasional beaching of whales and dolphins that occurs along the Cape coastline even today.

Cape Natives celebrated a special day in honor of Granny Squannit marked with offerings of food and ceremonial dances. She was particularly associated with the native cranberry, which the Wampanoags called sassamanesh. Eaten raw or cooked

Statue of Cummaquid Sachem Iyanough at the Hyannis Village Green, on Main Street in the heart of the village named for the Native. Photo: Jack Sheedy.

into a sauce, sassamanesh was sometimes mixed with venison to create pemmican, a protein-rich food. The Natives considered the berries a gift from their Great Spirit and cared for by Granny Squannit to assure a bountiful harvest. At harvest time it was customary to offer up a basket of the cranberries, which would be left at the marsh for Squannit to take as a token of their appreciation.

Vikings Visit Vinland

There is a place in history where fact and folklore become intermingled and entwined to the point where folklore may include remnants of fact, and vice versa. Such is the case with Norse sagas of the exploration of North America – to a place called Vinland – sometime around 1000 A.D., and the notion that this fabled Vinland was, in fact, the peninsula of Cape Cod.

Consider Cape Cod one thousand years ago, a vast wilderness of forests, untamed, brimming with animals and vegetation. It was, perhaps, an Eden with lush woodlands, cascading dunes, and waves crashing upon lonely beaches for mile after unbroken mile. The summers were warm but not oppressive, the autumns were cool and colorful, and the winters were relatively mild with an occasional storm. It seemed the perfect place for a group of voyagers from more northern and colder climes to settle.

According to Norse sagas, Vinland was discovered in 989 A.D. by a Viking explorer named Bjarni Herjulfsson. He left Iceland and neighboring Greenland, passing three landmasses along his journey. The first was Newfoundland. Next, he passed Nova Scotia. Sailing southwestward, he arrived at a third piece of land, believed to be Cape Cod. For reasons unknown he decided not to make landfall. Returning to Iceland he told of his journey and of the new worlds he discovered. Amongst those who would later hear the tales was Leif Erikson, son of Erik the Red, who was only eleven years old when Herjulfsson made his historic voyage.

For more than a decade no one ventured southwestward along Herjulfsson's path. The greatest discovery of any era – the discovery of a New World – was nearly overlooked, existing only within the sagas spoken at the village gatherings to keep the memories alive. Yet, around the year 1000 A.D., Leif Erikson became interested in the idea of seeking out and exploring this New World. Recently converted to Christianity, he felt it was his mission to sail to new lands, such as Greenland, to spread his newfound religion. He obtained a vessel and a crew and departed Iceland for whatever rested ahead. Stopping at Greenland to convert the population there, Leif followed Herjulfsson's path, taking him past Newfoundland, which he named Helluland for the mountains of ice and snow, and Nova Scotia, which he named Markland for its rich forests of trees, arriving at Cape Cod in September.

Into Nantucket Sound the Vikings sailed. The saga tells that Leif and his crew first landed at an island resting just north of another landmass, with a cape off to the north. Great Point, on the island of Nantucket, fits that description. Here they went ashore for a short period and noted that the dew in the grass tasted sweet, like honey. Back aboard ship, they sailed across the sound. The sagas tell that they came to a river that flows down from a lake. Bass River is such a river that lies just northwest of Great Point. At low tide, the ship became grounded at the mouth of the river, but when the tide turned the ship was lifted free and up the river the Vikings ventured. Erikson navigated his vessel the length of Bass River, some five miles into the heart of Cape Cod, to Follins Pond, which today separates Dennis and Yarmouth. Here he anchored, went ashore, and built shelter.

The Norse expedition spent the winter at the settlement on Follins Pond. Come spring, they departed for Greenland and Iceland beyond. It is believed that Leif Erikson never returned to his Vinland. Yet, tales of Leif Erikson's voyage to Vinland were retold again and again amongst the icebound Greenlanders. In the spring of the following year, Leif's brother Thorwald wished to try his luck in the New World. Arriving at Leif's camp on Follins Pond, the group was immediately struck by misfortune. The weather was horrible, the fish were not biting, and hunting was even less fruitful. The band of settlers began to doubt the wonderful stories of Vinland they had heard all the previous winter. After a time, the stormy weather abated, and fish and game stocks grew plentiful.

The sagas suggest that Thorwald and his crew explored the peninsula. They sailed around Monomoy Island and up the outer coastline of the Cape to Provincetown where the ship suffered a damaged keel on the shoals. Repairs were made, the ship was re-keeled, and Thorwald had the old keel timbers erected at the beach there, naming the land "Keelness." They then rounded the tip and entered Cape Cod Bay, sailing to what is now Bass Hole where they discovered a small band of Natives on the beach. Fearing they would alert more of their tribe to the Vikings' presence, Thorwald had them killed. But one escaped the massacre and ran off to warn the tribe. Soon Thorwald and his men were attacked by a much larger group of Natives. Thorwald took an arrow in the chest and fell to the sand, mortally wounded. He asked that he be buried there on the beach and, being Christian, asked that the men erect a cross at the head and foot of his grave.

The men called the place where Thorwald was buried "Crossness."

Thorwald's expedition remained on Vinland for two years before departing for Greenland. The next Norse expedition took place around 1007 A.D., with three ships, 165 men and women, and as much livestock as the ships could carry. Thus began the first attempted colonization of the Americas, spearheaded by Viking Thorfinn, his wife Gudrid, and Leif Erikson's half-sister, Freydis, and her husband. They arrived in summer and instantly succeeded in taming the land to their purposes. They were able to hunt and fish and occasionally capture a whale. During the following year the Norse made contact with the Natives and a peaceful meeting transpired and trade between the two groups commenced.

Later that year, Gudrid gave birth to a son. Named Snorri, he is considered the first European child to be born in the New World. Shortly afterwards the Natives returned to barter, but the meeting ended in disaster when a Native was accused of stealing one of the Vikings' weapons and was subsequently killed. Natives returned later by canoe in greater numbers. A battle ensued and, as the sagas relate, the frightened Norse were saved by Freydis, who picked up a sword from a dead Viking laying nearby and did battle with a number of Natives, inspiring the other Norse to rally to victory. Despite the victory, Thorfinn sensed that his dream of a Vinland settlement was not to be. Fear of attack became an everyday risk. And now their own society was beginning to break down as men grossly outnumbered the women, a cause for great concern amongst those without a partner. After nearly four years, the group loaded up their vessels, abandoned their settlement, and departed for Greenland.

The very next year, around 1011 A.D., talk began once again of a Vinland settlement. Two Icelandic brothers, Helgi and Finnborgi, heard the stories of a warmer land resting to the southwest and decided to give it a try. Meanwhile, Freydis learned of the brothers' plan and joined the expedition. Upon arrival the two groups instantly distrusted one another and settled in different areas. One evening, the men of Freydis' camp raided the other camp where they killed Helgi and Finnborgi and all the rest of the men in their sleep, while Freydis butchered the camp's five women with an axe.

That next spring, Freydis decided she had seen enough of the New

World. The Vikings sailed back to Greenland, thus ending the saga of the Eden-like Vinland. The Norse never succeeded in conquering this New World. We may never know if the peninsula of Cape Cod was the Vikings' Vinland. Archaeological evidence is certainly lacking. If Leif Erikson did arrive at North America a thousand years ago there were hundreds of rivers from Florida to Nova Scotia up which he could have sailed to make his settlement. Saga evidence seems to favor Cape Cod as its latitude matches the vague latitudinal inferences in the sagas. But until a rune stone is unearthed bearing the inscription "Leif Erikson was here, 1000 A.D." we may never know for sure.

Cape's Christopher Columbus

The year 2002 marked the 400th anniversary of a significant event in Cape Cod history, one that saw the first English explorer step foot upon these shores. In fact, it was an event that led to the naming of this place for its plentiful codfish.

English explorer Bartholomew Gosnold was nothing less than Cape Cod's Christopher Columbus. Born in 1571 into an influential family at Suffolk, England – one of nine children – he was the son of Anthony Gosnold, a lawyer, and Dorothy Bacon, whose ancestry included Francis Bacon. Family connections and wealth would help Gosnold later when he applied for patents to explore the New World.

While at college Gosnold became interested in tales of voyages and attended lectures and read texts on the subject. His later marriage to Mary Golding, the daughter of a lawyer and granddaughter of London's Lord Mayor, helped to introduce Gosnold to many influential people. In a career move, Gosnold became a successful privateer who sacked a number of Spanish vessels and ports during Britain's war with Spain. Gosnold's successes had gained him a favorable reputation. When Queen Elizabeth offered patents to open up trade routes to the East Indies, Gosnold's connections helped him to become chosen as captain of the bark *Concord* with a mission to build a trading post in the New World. He and his crew were also to search for valuable resources, document the flora and fauna, test the soils, and determine whether a permanent settlement could be established.

Leaving Falmouth, England in April 1602, the Atlantic crossing was relatively uneventful, though it is believed that Gosnold discovered the Gulf Stream. The vessel reached the coast of Maine by mid-May and within days Gosnold and his men encountered Natives. During a friendly meeting on board the *Concord*, one of the Natives drew a map of the coastline on the deck of the ship, a map showing the outline of Cape Cod.

Gosnold sailed south to the tip of the Cape, anchoring at Provincetown Harbor. There he and some of his men went ashore, becoming the first Englishmen to set foot in New England. At Provincetown the crew caught a number of codfish, prompting Gosnold to rename the landmass from Shoal Hope (his first choice) to Cape Cod.

Gosnold continued south around Monomoy and into Nantucket Sound, following the coastline until he reached an island where he went ashore. The explorer named this island – so rich in grape vines – for his daughter, Martha.

After leaving Martha's Vineyard, he explored a chain of islands nearby, and one in particular that appeared to be an ideal spot to set up a trading post. He called it Elizabeth Island (now Cuttyhunk Island, as the entire chain is now known as the Elizabeth Islands). On that island Gosnold had the men construct their encampment.

One spring day, a group of Natives paddled from the peninsula out to the island. The thirty or so Englishmen dined with more than fifty Natives in a Thanksgiving-type affair. Gosnold wrote in a letter to his father of the Native people's disposition: "The inhabitants there ... being of tall stature, comely proportion, strong, active, and some of good years, and as it should seem very healthful, are sufficient proof of the healthfulness of the place."

Although the original plan was to establish a permanent settlement, with a number of men staying behind while the *Concord* sailed for England to collect more men and fresh supplies, the crew decided against it. After just one month in the New World, the *Concord* set sail, arriving back at England by late July.

Although Gosnold never returned to Cape Cod, he was a key participant in the settlement of Jamestown, Virginia in 1607, commanding one of the expedition's three ships – the *God Speed*. Like a number of the settlers, he died of illness during the first year and was buried in the soil of the New World.

Martin Pring: A Forgotten Cape Explorer

A Cape explorer that is often omitted from the history books is Martin Pring, a man characterized by one historian as "the last of the Elizabethan seamen." Sandwiched as he was between Bartholomew Gosnold's 1602 expedition and the arrival of Samuel Champlain in 1605, it has always been difficult to pinpoint where Pring made landfall in this region. Some have him landing on Martha's Vineyard a year after Gosnold. Others have Pring scouting Plymouth Harbor. More recent scholarship puts Pring's camp at the mouth of the Pamet River in Truro and there is evidence to support this theory. A 1610 map connected to one of Pring's English backers shows his explorations to be near Provincetown. The "Whitson's Bay" location is a close approximation to the anchorage that Pring described in his journal. And his description of what the land looked like appears more consistent with the Outer Cape than it does to either the Vineyard or Plymouth.

Perhaps the best evidence of Pring's encampment being in Truro comes from William Bradford's journal where he mentions the Pilgrim scouting party finding "the remainder of an old fort, or palisade, which we conceived had been made by some Christians." Pring had described how his men built what he called a "baricado" for their protection. They had used it for seven weeks while gathering sassafras, one of the objects of their voyage. The water depth in the lower end of Pamet River would have been sufficient for Pring's two small vessels. And seventeen years after Pring's group had built their small fort, the remains would have still been there for the Pilgrims to see. Finally, the fact that neither Champlain nor Captain John Smith, both of whom had visited Plymouth and had made good maps of that place, mentioned the "baricado" would indicate that Pring hadn't set up his camp there.

So, we are left with the fact that an early explorer who was the only one to spend an extended time actually living on Cape Cod prior to the Pilgrims is the least known. That explorer was Martin Pring.

A Pointed Rear Guard Action

In October of 1606, after navigating around what he called "Cape Mallebare," the treacherous Pollack Rip Shoal, French explorer Samuel de Champlain arrived in Chatham's Stage Harbor. He named it "Port

Fortune." It was not the first visit to Cape Cod by the explorer as he had spent the preceding summer charting the New England coastline while searching for a site to found a warmer version of New France. Champlain anchored in Nauset Harbor that previous year and was impressed with the landscape that he observed. He made extensive and accurate drawings of the area with the full intention of returning to establish a colony.

"Port Fortune" did not, however, prove to be good fortune for Champlain. Relations with the Native people turned sour after it appeared that they were making themselves too familiar with the French supplies. A bloody fight ensued wherein several of Champlain's men were killed. The French were forced to retreat to their ship.

Without a corresponding written account by the Natives, it is probably wrong to simply accept the French version of where the guilt for the conflict rested, but the Native people showed their contempt for the retreating Europeans in a particularly rude manner. They repeatedly dug up the bodies of the dead Frenchmen and tore down the cross that had been placed on the gravesite. In addition, as Champlain described their behavior in his journal, the Natives exhibited their contempt toward the French, "Turning their backs toward the barque (ship), they did cast sand with their two hands betwixt their buttocks in derision, howling like wolves."

The image is pretty clear. It would appear that Champlain and his crew were "mooned" by the Natives, the first and certainly not the last recorded case of such an insult directed at tourists in the history of Cape Cod.

Squanto's Sad End

Squanto's arrival in Plimoth in the spring of 1621 was seen by the Pilgrims as being "a special instrument sent of God for their good beyond their expectation." And it is true that he played a vital role in their ability to adapt to their new surroundings.

But Squanto's place in Pilgrim history is actually rather clouded. In fact, his star rose and fell quickly. Just a year later when he died, the man who had acted as the helpful intermediary between the Pilgrims and the Wampanoags was accorded neither a resting place within the English community that he had adopted, nor among the sacred burial places of his own people.

Squanto, or Tisquantum as he was known by his Native compatriots, had been captured on Cape Cod by English Captain Thomas Hunt in 1614. He was taken to Spain and from what we know, was sold there as a servant. Somehow he ended up in England and was eventually taken by fishermen to the coast of Maine. From there, he walked back to the region that his tribe had inhabited near Plimoth. When he got there, he found that a pestilence had killed all of the members of his tribe. He took refuge with Massasoit, then sachem of the Wampanoags. When Massasoit learned of the arrival of the Pilgrims, he directed Squanto to present himself and assist these Englishmen.

Massasoit had reasons for doing this. Facing a large and vigorous tribe of Narragansetts to his west, Massasoit desired the military power of the English to protect his tribe from the incursions of his more aggressive neighbors. He knew that if he could convince the Pilgrims that there was a mutual interest in keeping the Narragansetts on the defensive, then his own tribe would benefit. Largely through Squanto's efforts, the Wampanoags were able to enlist the Pilgrims as an ally and a peace treaty was signed by both parties pledging to aid each other in the case of trouble.

Squanto apparently tried to make himself far more important in the grand scheme of things than either the Pilgrims or Massasoit had envisioned. Believing that the debt the Pilgrims owed him for their survival during that first year made him essential to them, he began to exact small payments of various sort from them. And he did the same to his Native compatriots. As William Bradford later put it, "… Squanto sought his own ends, and played his own game, by putting the Indians in fear and drawing gifts from them to enrich himself; making them believe that he could stir up war against whom he would, and make peace for whom he would."

Squanto claimed to have the power to release a plague on the Wampanoags, telling them he learned the secret from the Pilgrims. He also told his fellow Natives that he could control whether the Pilgrims would stay faithful as allies in the event of a war. Squanto's initial popularity and his continuing influence with the Pilgrims raised a powerful envy in Massasoit and the sachem made no secret that he would not be upset if Squanto suddenly disappeared from the scene. After Squanto allegedly initiated a false claim that Massasoit was planning to attack the Pilgrims, the Wampanoag leader demanded that the settlers turn him over for execution. They refused.

Realizing that he had overplayed his hand, Squanto stayed very close to the Pilgrims for protection. He claimed to have adopted Christianity and continued to act as a guide and interpreter while the English explored the areas around Plimoth and Cape Cod. In the fall of 1622, while guiding the Pilgrims near Chatham, Squanto became ill and died. Bradford described the death of his Native friend thusly. "In this place Squanto fell sick of an Indian fever, bleeding much at the nose, and within a few days, died there desiring that we pray for him that he might go to the Englishman's God in heaven." Pray for him they no doubt did, but the body of Squanto was not buried in Plimoth, nor was it given a place of honor among his own people. Instead, his remains lie in an unmarked and uncelebrated grave somewhere at the Cape's foggy elbow.

Chapter 2

At Work

Cape Codders were no strangers to hard work. Whether it was farming, or fishing, or whaling, or hauling cargoes along the coast, or sailing clipper ships to foreign ports, or working in a mill, or in a factory, it was all an honest day's work for an honest day's pay. Many did go to sea to earn their living, but others stayed on dry land, working in their hometown and contributing to their daily village life. And still others left the Cape to present their ideas and their wares on the larger national stage, some finding success and others not so much.

Inventive Cape Codders

Cape Cod has produced a surprising number of people whose ideas contributed to new ways of getting things done. Call them inventors, or entrepreneurs, or even opportunists, these people seized upon an idea with the intention of making both an improvement in a process or product and, hopefully, a lot of money. Most of these ideas and businesses never had an impact further than the villages of their origin, but several graduated beyond the Cape to have national importance.

Gustavus Swift, for example, whose roots went back to nineteenth century Sandwich, eventually took his skills at bartering livestock to Chicago and founded Swift and Company, one of the great meat packing companies of the country. In the early nineteenth century the Winslow family of Brewster built a fulling mill in the west section of town that is said to have produced the first factory-made woolen cloth in America. The factory model was copied and transferred to other New England mill sites. Caleb Chase of West Harwich decided not to follow his many brothers to sea and, instead, concentrated on the emerging coffee importation business, developing a fortune as a partner in the well-known Chase and Sanborn "coffee empire." Still another Cape Codder, Samuel Mayo Nickerson, left his native Chatham and carried his financial skills to the Midwest, becoming president of the First National Bank of Chicago.

Perhaps typical of the kinds of inventive activity and entrepreneurial spirit associated with business that went on in Cape towns is the example of Harwich. In the mid-nineteenth century the town boasted a soap factory, a tanning business, and a plant for the manufacturing of fishermen's boots and men's and ladies' slippers. A barrel factory was constructed to serve the needs of the growing cranberry industry in the town and there was a shirt and overall factory built in 1865 that employed as many as two hundred and fifty people. A cotton and woolen factory, a boiler plant, and a tap and die factory were also part of Harwich's nineteenth century industrial past.

Hyannis was another center for new products. Mabel Kimball Baker started the Colonial Candle Company in her kitchen by making traditional hand-dipped candles from the bayberry bushes that are found throughout the Cape. She began her enterprise by selling candles from the porch of her house. In 1910, she received a small order from a Boston retail company that was given a sample of her candles by a summer visitor. The product sold well and the initial order was repeated and increased. Sensing that she struck on something, she and her husband, Walter D. Baker, pooled their resources and built a factory in Hyannis to mass-produce the popular candles. By the 1920s, the candle company was selling millions of candles throughout the nation.

Another Hyannis inventor and entrepreneur was Mr. Edward Petow who developed an unusual process of using herring scales to provide the luster for artificial pearls. During the First World War, Mr. Petow began experimenting with chemicals that would bind the scales to the glass beads that were used as the pearls. The glass beads were then dipped in the silvery liquid to acquire the sheen that made them unique and highly prized. Locally, the pearls were marketed as "Priscilla Pearls" and they were very successful. It was said that the finished product was indistinguishable from the real thing and only the best experts and chemical analysis could detect it from the genuine pearl. The business thrived until overseas competition and the eventual depressed economy of the 1930s ended production.

In the west end of Hyannis Doctor Samuel Pitcher produced a homeopathic elixir called "Castoria." As with most inventors, Pitcher claimed his product contained a secret formula. Included along with pumpkin seed, peppermint, bicarbonate soda, and sugar was a healthy dose of alcohol. The product was marketed as a cure for such nineteenth century problems as dyspepsia, dropsy, dysentery, and "summer complaints."

Eventually, Doctor Pitcher's product attracted the attention of Mr. Charles Fletcher of New York City. Fletcher Brothers was a well-known name in the types of herbal medicines that were being sold around the Northeast at that time. In 1869, Pitcher sold his Castoria formula to Fletcher's company for ten thousand dollars. Within a very short time, Fletcher Brothers created one of the longest marketed and best-selling health remedies in American history. Under the slogan "Children cry for it," Fletcher's Castoria became the most popular elixir sold anywhere in the country.

These examples of creative Cape Codders who played on the wider national stage were paralleled by hundreds of individuals whose ideas had local, if often only temporary, impact. The short-lived Provincetown skunk farm of the late nineteenth century, an enterprise that produced skunks for both meat and fur, selling the pelts for between four and six dollars apiece, was such an example. Falmouth's early twentieth century attempt to become the mushroom growing capital of the nation was ended when the Gifford Street op-

Valentine Doane's baby carriage wasn't a big seller. Source: U.S. Patent Office

eration was wiped out by a persistent blight that closed the business after only a few years.

Valentine Doane, Jr. of Harwich patented a baby carriage in the 1880s that never caught the public's attention. Joseph Cummings and William Howes operated a clothing manufacturing business in Orleans that produced Plymouth Rock Pants. Unfortunately, the pants never became as well-known as the famous rock and the business failed. Even the promising "Queen Anne Commode," produced by the Harwich Port Manufacturing Company in the late nineteenth century, did not achieve much of a following.

One thing is still certain. Today's entrepreneurs have learned that a product that carries the name of Cape Cod attached to it generally has a good chance to sell. Cape Codders continue to create and exploit new markets, proving that the inventive spirit remains very much with us still.

Great Marshes of West Barnstable

Cape Codders from centuries ago harvested the lands and the seas to form their very existence. They eagerly accepted what the Cape had to offer. In those days nothing was wasted, everything had value. For instance, they collected seaweed from the beaches during late summer and fall to "bank up," or insulate the foundations of their homes against the frigid winter winds to come.

For those Cape Codders who farmed and owned livestock, earning their living from the soil rather than from the sea, a certain feature of the Cape played an important role in their daily agrarian existence. Livestock required hay for fodder and bedding. As the crop yield from Cape soil was much less than what farmers were used to harvesting inland, therefore requiring more land to produce the same yield, it was impractical use of the land to devote much of it to the cultivation of hay. The Cape environment, though, provided a natural solution to satisfy this need.

The Great Marsh running along the northern edges of West Barnstable yielded vast amounts of salt hay. This salt hay, though somewhat inferior to regular hay in terms of nutritional content and taste, provided adequate fodder and bedding for the Cape's livestock. The early settlers quickly realized the value of Barnstable's marshlands,

Harvesting salt hay on West Barnstable's Great Marshes. Photo courtesy of the Commonwealth of Massachusetts Department of Labor and Industries, 1922.

one of the largest tidal marshes on the Massachusetts coastline, some eight thousand acres in area. Though settlement began in the eastern part of Barnstable near the harbor, then called Mattakeese, a number of families from Scituate relocated to what was then called the settlement of Great Marshes, now known as the village of West Barnstable. The soil at Great Marshes, just south of the hay grounds, was considered to be some of the richest on the peninsula. And the marshes provided all the hay they would ever need.

Initially, the salt marshes across Cape Cod were available to the local farmers of the area on the rather informal basis known as common ownership. A farmer and workers simply went to the marsh-lands and took what they needed. But, as the population grew and the number of farmers requiring hay expanded, the towns found it necessary to divide up the salt marshes and draw up legal rights of ownership. Much bickering commenced over these valuable lands as the ownership of salt marsh acreage became both important to farmers and profitable to those who went into the business of selling hay to farmers.

Inland, the cultivation of hay occurred during June and July, during the period that maximized nutritional content, digestibility, and curing, while in the salt marshes of the Cape the hay was harvested during the lowest possible tides in the month of August, plain and simple. Harvested salt hay would be piled on staddles – platforms built of planks atop posts planted into the marsh – in order to keep the reaped grasses dry above the tidal seawater. Such a harvest as this was a race against the tides, bad weather, and the pesky green head flies that frequented the marshes during the heat of August.

At one time, prior to the 20th century, the great salt marshes of Barnstable contained thousands of staddles elevating the salt hay harvest of an entire town above the damaging waters of high tide. Yet, haymaking from salt marshes petered out during the latter years of the nineteenth century as the Cape Codders' diet was being provided more and more by off-Cape farmers now that the railroad firmly connected the peninsula to the mainland. Left to the elements, the staddles eventually fell to a century's worth of storms.

The Glint of Sandwich Glass

Deming Jarves, a Bostonian involved in the glass making business, visited Sandwich in 1824 for a vacation of hunting and fishing. The previous year his father had died, leaving him with money which he planned to use toward realizing his dream of revolutionizing the glass making industry. While in Sandwich, Jarves noticed the sandy beaches and the thick woodlands. He began to consider the notion of building a glass factory in this Cape Cod setting where the sand to make the glass was to be found in vast quantities and the trees to fuel the furnaces grew all around. The very next year he opened his Boston and Sandwich Glass Works at Factory and Harbor streets.

Unfortunately, Sandwich sand contained too much iron for glass-making. No matter, Jarves arranged to have sand shipped in from as far away as Florida. And so, Sandwich became a factory town as the glass-making operation commenced and chimneys belched black smoke into the skies. The glass factory met with instant success. Sales tripled in the span of four years, from $32,000 in 1827 to $93,000 in 1830. The operation was a boon to the Sandwich economy, employing around five hundred people in 1850 and creating a number of peripheral jobs. A lumber company was established to cut the trees in a 2,000-acre forest to feed the fires. A transportation system was put into place. Housing was built around the factory for the skilled workers. Jarves even had his own steamship built because he became fed up with the railroad's fees. Soon the company was putting out a half-ton's worth of glassware each week, $600,000 worth of glassware annually.

Jarves' factory produced the country's first pressed and laced glass. Besides creating artistic glassware the company also produced basic glassware products that could be used by the average person in their daily life. Whether tumblers, plates,

Deming Jarves, the founder of the Boston and Sandwich Glass Company. Courtesy of the Sandwich Glass Museum.

salt shakers, lamps, bowls, or candleholders, the use of automation and molds made the glassware affordable. Yet, at the same time the company created some of the most exquisite pieces in the world and experimented with different shades of color to create works of art unmatched anywhere. Jarves covered both ends of the spectrum, from the artistic to the practical.

Over the span of a quarter century Sandwich became one of the most successful towns on the Cape. After thirty-three years, though, Jarves resigned to start another glass company that he planned to hand down to his son, John, who worked along with him. Opened in 1864, Jarves' new venture was called Cape Cod Glass Works, but misfortune struck when John died and Jarves ultimately lost the will to continue. Within five years, he, too, was dead.

Boston and Sandwich Glass continued on without its founder. With the Civil War behind them, the glassmakers of Sandwich looked forward to the prosperity to follow. And prosperous times did indeed follow the company into the 1880s, but a series of events sounded the death knell. First, in 1884, the town of Sandwich split up; the villages of Bourne, Buzzards Bay, Cataumet, Pocasset, Sagamore, and Monument Beach became the town of Bourne. The tax base of Sandwich was essentially cut in half with the division. Meanwhile, competition sprung up out in the Midwest in the form of other glassmakers producing affordable glassware. Their furnaces were fired by less expensive and inexhaustible natural gas rather than by wood. Other East Coast glass companies made the move out west, but Boston and Sandwich resisted.

Ultimately, a strike resulting from a wage dispute at the factory finished off the glass works for good. Once work stopped and the furnaces went cold they were never fired up again. A number of attempts to reopen the factory failed and Sandwich, suffering from crippling unemployment, fell into a great depression. The closing of the glass works sent out a ripple that devastated other businesses in the town. It took many decades for Sandwich to recover.

In its sixty-year run, Boston and Sandwich Glass Works produced about $30 million worth of glass. Its products found their way into homes across the country and to every foreign port where America's ships sailed. Today, Sandwich glass is prized by collectors and admirers, alike.

Banana Appeal

Jamaica, with a quarter of its labor force working in the field of agriculture, lists bananas as one of its chief crops and major exports. That industry and its century-long banana trade can be traced to the efforts of a Cape Cod man who saw an opportunity within those slippery yellow peels.

Captain Lorenzo Dow Baker of Wellfleet arrived at Jamaica in 1870 on board the schooner *Telegraph* to pick up a cargo of bamboo. As he was making his pickup he had his men take on a supply of bananas. His plan was to transport them north to Boston to see if there was any interest in the fruit. Yet, by the time the ship had arrived only as far north as the Carolinas the fruit spoiled and was cast overboard.

Baker was in Jamaica again the next year. This time he took a supply of green bananas and was successful in delivering them to Boston before they had a chance to spoil. The fruit was well-received by consumers and as a result the wheels began to turn in his head. He established the L. D. Baker Company to move cargoes of fruit from tropical places to American ports. That company became the Boston Fruit Company, and later, the United Fruit Company.

For a number of years Baker split his time between his Cape Cod home in Wellfleet and his adopted second home on Jamaica. In Wellfleet he built the Chequesset Inn in 1885, a grand hotel that was situated out over the waters at Wellfleet Harbor. Meanwhile, in Jamaica he dabbled in ways of promoting the island and its exports to off-island interests, bringing economic prosperity both as a tourist destination and a grower of exotic fruits and useable natural resources.

The island of Jamaica never forgot the man who helped to improve its economy. A 1905 ceremony held on the island to commemorate the then 65-year old Baker celebrated the fact that he'd done more for Jamaica in thirty years "than the British Empire in three hundred years."

In 1908, Lorenzo Dow Baker, Cape Cod's "Banana King," slipped the tethers of earth for the heavenly sphere.

Penzance Point's Pungent Product

Penzance Point in Woods Hole is one of Falmouth's most exclusive developments. In the early part of the 20th century the area became an exclusive home away from home for New York bankers and wealthy Boston socialites. It is the sort of place that exemplifies the finest in Cape Cod living styles.

In the second half of the nineteenth century, this section of Falmouth was anything but a setting for the affluent. It was the working-class district of the town and a decidedly blue-collar zone inhabited by Irish workers who toiled in the odorous service of the thriving Pacific Guano Company. Anyone with nasal sensitivities avoided Woods Hole.

The guano industry was, for a time in the 1800s, the most important employer in Falmouth. The business was started on Long Neck in 1863 and utilized the bird droppings that were shipped there for processing from islands in the Caribbean and Pacific. The need for organic fertilizer was growing both in the United States and Europe, and the Pacific Guano Company entered an expanding market in a time of great demand. With its headquarters in Boston and additional

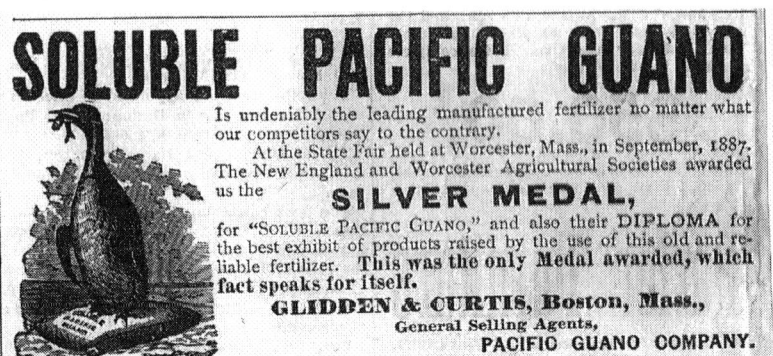

SOLUBLE PACIFIC GUANO

Is undeniably the leading manufactured fertilizer no matter what our competitors say to the contrary.

At the State Fair held at Worcester, Mass., in September, 1887. The New England and Worcester Agricultural Societies awarded us the

SILVER MEDAL,

for "SOLUBLE PACIFIC GUANO," and also their DIPLOMA for the best exhibit of products raised by the use of this old and reliable fertilizer. **This was the only Medal awarded, which fact speaks for itself.**

GLIDDEN & CURTIS, Boston, Mass.,
General Selling Agents,
PACIFIC GUANO COMPANY.

Glidden & Curtis acted as general s(m)elling agents for the Pacific Guano Company's odorous product.

facilities in Beaufort and Charleston, South Carolina, the enterprise employed more than thirty ships to bring the odorous ingredients to Woods Hole for processing.

The actual process of converting the guano to fertilizer involved mixing decaying fish, amply supplied by local fishermen, and sulfur with the guano. The natural phosphate contained in the bird droppings combined with the nitrogen in the fish to produce an effective, if malodorous, commercial fertilizer. The company used Great Harbor as its shipping point, and on some occasions more than a dozen vessels would be loading near Ram Island. As the business grew, the need for efficient land transportation encouraged the building of the Woods Hole branch of the Old Colony Railroad in 1872. Horse-drawn wagons hauled tons of fertilizer to the waiting rail cars off Luscombe Avenue.

The company failed suddenly in February of 1889, due in large part to mismanagement rather than because of lack of demand for its product. It appears that someone on the management side was playing fast and loose with receipts while "cooking the books" for the auditors. When a Lynn, Massachusetts bank called in its loan, the company was short of cash and couldn't make the payment. In what one company official called a case of "pure cussedness," the bank sent County Sheriff Alfred Crocker into the plant to seize the assets and padlock the facility. More than one hundred workers lost their jobs in the closure. Some 40,000 tons of processed fertilizer awaited shipment to eager customers. Although this inventory was eventually sold, the company never opened again.

The factory itself was torn down in 1894. A little more than a decade later the first large estates were carved from the land on Penzance Point and today, perhaps with the exception of some extremely healthy gardens, there is nothing to even hint at what was once an important Cape Cod industry.

When a Cobb was a Coach

Brewster at one time had more sea captains than any other Cape Cod town. But Freeman Cobb, whose father was a famous master mariner, didn't follow that career path, achieving in his own right considerable fame and fortune on dry land. Cobb, born in 1831, instead took a job in New York City with Adams Express Company, an international freight service. At age 23, he was sent by the company to establish a transportation branch in Australia. At the time there was great excitement with the recent discovery of gold at "Forest Creek," in Victoria. There was a need for reliable transportation to and from the diggings. For some reason the Adams Company venture did not work out. Cobb persisted and with several partners from New England he founded Cobb & Co in 1854. The company's first run from Melbourne to Castlemaine was an immediate success.

With imported cutting-edge coaches from America and American drivers familiar with frontier conditions out west, Cobb and his partners established a virtual monopoly on transport of passengers, luggage, mining tools, and produce. The company was also able to win mail contracts and did gold escort work. Within two years Cobb & Co. was very successful and a stage coach was referred to as a "Cobb." After a few years Cobb sold out his interest in the company, realizing a profit of $32,000, a huge sum for that time. Under the directorship of other partners, Cobb & Co. became synonymous with efficient and reliable transportation across much of Australia. By the early 20th century, the company was the largest coaching system in the world with interests in mining and smelting as well as railroads.

Returning to Brewster, Cobb became active in politics, eventually becoming a state senator. He was a director of the Cape Cod Central Railroad, which was built in 1865. His new business ventures, however, never equaled the success he'd had in Australia. In 1871 he took his family to South Africa, hoping to set up a transportation system to the diamond mines at Kimberley. The firm eventually went into bankruptcy. Cobb, whose name became common use in the Australia language as a synonym for a coach, died insolvent in Port Elizabeth, South Africa in May of 1878.

A One-Man Telephone Company

Up until 1910, if a person in Orleans wanted to talk to someone in town he had to walk, get in a cart, or ride a horse to that person's house. But in that year Henry Knowles Cummings, a preeminent merchant, decided to do something about it. He became the founder and owner of the Orleans Telephone Company.

The New England Telephone Company was attempting to expand its territory on Cape Cod. They approached Cummings to help them open a franchise in Orleans. The company told Cummings that if he got five customers they would put a switchboard in an upstairs room in his store. Cummings found that it was so easy to get people to sign up that he decided to start his own company. The board of selectmen, acting as the licensing authority, awarded the telephone franchise to Cummings rather than to the larger New England Telephone Company. Cummings located a firm that sold a machine that would carry a human voice 100 miles. It cost $15.00. Since all of Orleans was about eight miles long, it was more than adequate. With his brother, George, Cummings cut down 125 cedar trees from a swamp behind the Masonic Hall. He used these for poles to string up his telephone wires. For $10.00 a year a subscriber could talk to anyone in Orleans. Soon "H.K.," as he was known around town, was making a lot of money.

The New England Telephone Company was persistent and eventually convinced Cummings to sell the telephone poles to them as they extended their own service in town. The contract said that Cummings could continue to use the poles for his wires. But shortly after, the New England Telephone people told him that while he could keep his wires on each pole, he could not use the space between them! It was a blatant attempt to put Cummings out of business. But Cummings wasn't a quitter. He produced a paper that showed that as a franchise owner he had the right to share use of telephone poles regardless of who actually owned them and that included the space between them.

The legal tussle went on for a couple of years until Cummings sold his operation to the larger company for a good profit. They agreed to rent a room up over his store where the telephone exchange was set up, paying him $80.00 a month for the space.

A number of customers didn't want to switch to the new company and they stayed with Cummings. He continued to collect their subscription fee. Years later, when Cummings' Orleans Phone Company was only a memory, Walter Mayo, one of his original customers in East Orleans, was still using two of Cummings' original phones to communicate from his house to his duck barn.

Italians on Strike

The Cape Cod Canal was opened in 1914. Yet, the first attempt at digging began in September of 1880 when Italian immigrants from New York arrived to toil for a number of weeks until a work stoppage resulted due to nonpayment of wages. These were troubled times in Sandwich with hundreds of disgruntled Italian workers wandering the streets of the small Cape Cod village.

Things began peacefully as documented in the September 20, 1880 issue of the *Barnstable Patriot*: "The work on the Cape Cod Ship Canal was commenced on Wednesday morning, Sept. 15th, by 150 Italians, who arrived in Sandwich from New York, on Tuesday …The digging, at present, is being done on what is called the 'Bodfish' field, belonging to William Fessenden, Esq., and is just west of the Town Neck crossing, and the dirt is taken off down to the water, wheeled out on both sides leaving a ditch 66 feet wide, which is to be the width of the canal at the bottom, the sides sloping back according to the height of the land."

It was important to get laborers in place moving earth since the charter for the Cape Cod Ship Canal Company stipulated that a significant expenditure toward construction be made by November 1, 1880, or else the competing Cape Cod Canal Company would receive the charter to dig the canal. More Italians arrived, with numbers ranging as high as four or five hundred moving a significant amount of terrain and digging down to groundwater. By mid-October, though, things went downhill quickly when the Italians had not been paid or fed. From the October 25th *Patriot*: "The Italians at work on the Cape Cod Canal, having received no money since they began work and

*Italian laborers start work on the Cape Cod Canal. September 1880.
Courtesy of the Bourne Historical Society*

promises having been several times broken, ceased work on Monday noon, and Tuesday noon gathered about the Central House, where the Sub Contractors were, and demanded their money."

No money was forthcoming despite promises made, leading to a dire situation involving several hundred angry, unpaid, hungry workers running amuck in a Cape Cod town ill-equipped to deal with the situation. A *Patriot* article dated November 1 provides further details: "The Italians at work on the Cape Cod Canal at Sandwich, becoming impatient and thoroughly disgusted at receiving no pay but promises for their month's work gathered again on Tuesday forenoon, just a week from their first outbreak, in front of the Central House, demanding satisfaction. The prospect of a serious disturbance was much greater than on the former occasion, as the men have been on strike for a week and were becoming exasperated." The Italian workers held a contractor's son as a bargaining chip, but he was soon released unharmed. Initially, local residents sided with the contractors against what they viewed as an unruly gang, but when they learned the reality of how the Italians had been wrongly treated they provided food for the unpaid and unfed workers.

Finally, the situation was resolved and the Italians were "shipped away in squads of sixty" back to New York. Thus, the curtain closed on the so-called "Neapolitan Revolt," or as the *Patriot* concludes, "This ends the attempt to dig the Cape Cod Canal under the present Company."

Chapter 3

At Sea

The lure of the sea reached out and snatched up many a Cape Cod man, some at an early age, enticing the sons of this peninsula to leave the relative comfort and security of their dry land homes behind for the mystery and the romance of the rising and falling tides. But not all voyages produced a predictable ending, and not all mariners were men. There were a number of women who went down to the sea in ships – mostly with their seafaring husbands – thus lending a different perspective on the business of navigating within Poseidon's briny realm.

Women Who Went to Sea

It is difficult to pass through a Cape Cod village without some reference to an important local shipmaster who put the place on the map. What is perhaps less known is that a lot of women from Cape Cod went to sea alongside their men. The adventures and experiences of these seafaring ladies are not generally found in the history books. Only recently have historians begun to examine the seagoing journals kept by women and these materials are adding another dimension to the picture of what life was like aboard ships.

In the 19th century, as American trading and whaling interests took ships and crews to far off places around the world, it became increasingly common for the wives of sea captains to accompany their husbands to foreign ports.

Like their husbands, these women experienced seasickness, mutinies, pirate attacks, storms, and shipwrecks. Often making their first voyages as newly married young women, the wives of shipmasters entered a

Persis Crowell Addy, wife of Captain John Addy, Master of the Clipper Ship Christopher Hall. *She survived an 1867 shipwreck off Samoa. Jim Carr Collection*

male-dominated culture where the presence of a female on a ship was often considered bad luck by many crewmembers.

The order of a ship was a pyramid-shaped structure where the captain took the top position followed by the descending hierarchy of mates and seamen. In that mix the position of the captain's wife was a tenuous and delicate one. Naturally near the top of the pyramid with her husband, she still had to be careful so as not to appear to eclipse his authority. Women who appeared to wield undue influence aboard a vessel could earn the ship the dubious title "hen frigate" from a superstitious crew.

Relations were always delicate between the captain's wife and the men who operated the ship. She could not appear too close to or yet become too distant from the ship's routine, lest the men begin to focus their own loneliness or frustrations on her. Often she was socially isolated and without the association of other females for long periods of time. Sailors could be particularly cruel if they took a dislike to the captain's wife.

"She is the meanest, most hoggish and the greediest female that has ever existed," one sailor wrote in reference to his captain's wife. "Her looks is despised by everyone on board and the whistle of a gale of wind through the rigging is much more musical than the sound of her voice."

For the woman who might have to serve as a surgeon, cook, and surrogate mother to young and undisciplined crewmembers it could be a lonely and often frustrating experience.

One wife commented on her ship's first mate, noting, "Without exception I think him nearest to a savage of anyone I have ever met. He possesses a very quick, ungovernable temper, is also very jealous and is very ignorant of the rules of good breeding. And yet he has a high opinion of himself!"

The captain and his wife and any children they might have with them lived in the aft cabin at the stern of the ship. The crew was billeted in the forecastle up forward and it was not expected that the men would enter the family quarters. The rules were described by one woman who wrote, "A strict code of etiquette is maintained aboard these ships. The second and third mates and carpenter are served at our table after we are through. The steward eats in the pantry; the cook in his galley. The men of the crew, and the boys, have their meals, in fine weather, on the forward part of the deck. Where there is a storm, they are served in their own quarters."

The nineteenth century sea journals of women are filled with remarks about constant seasickness, comments about strange and exotic foreign cultures, and references to the dangers of heavy weather. Forecasts were non-existent and vessels often found themselves in the teeth of tremendous gales. Mary Mathews Bray of Yarmouth, who was with her father aboard the ship *National Eagle*, described one stormy experience, noting, "It is difficult to write. I have to grasp my paper with one hand, my pen with the other, and brace my knees against the table, lest we all part company."

Georgianna Dyer, who sailed from Provincetown aboard the whaling schooner *Ellen A. Swift* with her husband Captain J. Emmons Dyer, found herself in a storm off the Hatteras whaling grounds. Her ship was so battered that she later compared the experience of being thrown around the cabin to that of being like a bowling ball.

Sally Mayo Lavender, also from Provincetown, recounted her experience of trying to sleep in a March Atlantic storm aboard the brig *Panama*. "I clung to the sides (of the berth) to prevent being thrown out and for a moment I am lost. I hardly know whether I am in the berth or on the floor."

In the Far East trade there was the particular danger of pirates. In 1865, off the coast of China, Mrs. Lucy Lord Howes of Dennis, who was aboard the small clipper *Lubra*, saw her husband, Captain Benjamin P. Howes, murdered by pirates in their cabin. Left for dead by the departing pirates who set the ship on fire, she was able, with the help of several surviving crewmen, to douse the flames and make repairs to the damaged ship, working it back to one of the Chinese treaty ports and safety.

Mary Connolly of Dennis was with her husband aboard the ship *South America* when it struck an uncharted reef off the coast of West Africa. As the ship began to break up, Mrs. Connolly was lashed to pieces of wreckage and with the survivors, floated to the barren and isolated coast. For several weeks before being rescued she experienced near starvation and the threat of hostile natives.

Women who visited foreign ports were exposed to cultures that those who remained at home could hardly imagine. From the foot binding practices of China to exotic foods and unusual birds, Cape women brought back memories of fascinating foreign adventures while aboard ship. Young Alice Baxter of South Dennis recalled seeing the effects of the 1883 explosion of the volcano Krakatoa on a voyage out to China aboard the ship *Obed Baxter*.

In recounting the tales of seafaring women, it would seem reasonable to assume that they were the "liberated women" of the nineteenth century. But this assessment would not be accurate. The motives of women who went to sea with their husbands were anything but radical. Rather than an opportunity for breaking new social ground, most seagoing women accepted their role as being both expected and necessary. They saw the experience as part of preserving a traditional marriage and they acted as supportive helpmates and partners to their husbands.

But the sight of American ships headed for home from foreign ports would often induce pangs of loneliness for the comfort of land-bound extended families far away. Sally Mayo Lavender summed up the mixed feelings of most seagoing women when she wrote in her journal, "I felt rather a tinge of homesickness tonight. But homesickness I could not call it for this is all the home I know at present; for here are my all: husband and child; but felt isolated."

In much the same vein, Sandwich's Hannah Burgess wrote, "Once in no other place than my native town could I be happy. No other friends could please me but my parents and relatives. Now where my husband is, there is my home. May it ever be thus."

John Adams' Other Abigail

With its sandy arm that reaches out into the Atlantic, Cape Cod harbors its share of mysteries. The foggy tale of the *Abigail* is one such mystery that makes as little sense today as it did in 1772. It is a tale that was so talked about in its day that colonial Governor Thomas Hutchinson was among those who presided over its court case while Boston lawyer and future US President John Adams defended the accused. It would not be Adams' first controversial court case, as he earlier defended the British troops who fired on an angry mob in 1770, killing five townspeople in what would become known as the Boston Massacre.

This latest case involved a Chatham man – Ansel Nickerson – the sole survivor of an apparent massacre on board the schooner *Abigail* off the coast of Cape Cod. The vessel was discovered by Captain Joseph Doane, Jr. on November 15, 1772, adrift off Chatham with only one man aboard and evidence of damage in the form of a barrel of rum broken open. Nickerson, the sole crewmember, was found in a state of distress and was described by Doane as being quite frightened.

Nickerson told a tale that began with the *Abigail* leaving Boston Harbor for a journey across Massachusetts Bay and down the outer coast of the Cape to Chatham, and concluded with claims of piracy, plunder, kidnap, and murder. On board the vessel along with Nickerson had been two cousins, Thomas Nickerson and Sparrow Nickerson, their brother-in-law Elisha Newcomb, and a thirteen-year old boy named William Kent, Jr. In the early morning of that November day, according to Ansel Nickerson's testimony, a British schooner emerged from the darkness and came alongside the *Abigail*. Afraid that he would be impressed to serve aboard the British vessel, Nickerson hid out of sight, hanging from a rope over the side of the ship.

According to the sole survivor, the British pirates murdered the two Nickerson men and Newcomb, stole some of the ship's cargo, and then kidnapped the young Kent boy. After they left, Nickerson climbed back on board the *Abigail* where he was discovered by Captain Doane. The vessel was towed to port and Doane reported the events to the authorities in Barnstable. Nickerson's story, though, did not seem to add up. A search for a pirate vessel of Nickerson's description was conducted, but no such vessel was found. All eyes shifted to the Chatham man as the perpetrator of the terrible murders. He was arrested and taken away to Boston for trial.

John Adams was selected to defend Nickerson. Even beforehand, the Braintree lawyer was already thinking and writing in his journal about the bizarre event off Cape Cod, describing it as "a mysterious, inexplicable affair." Adams' eyebrows must have raised a bit as he considered the events surrounding the case, for the plundered vessel shared the name of his own wife – Abigail.

Meanwhile, Nickerson's story became more and more unbelievable. Captain Doane's testimony did not mention the bloody decks that Nickerson had described. Was the Admiralty Court to believe that three men could be butchered without a drop of blood? And what happened to the bodies? If they were tossed overboard in the vicinity of Chatham they would have washed up on a beach. Even the damage to the ship as reported by Nickerson was not corroborated by Captain Doane's testimony. The only piece of evidence that Doane would corroborate was that a barrel of rum was broken into and was left with only a few gallons of the liquor remaining. Other than that, all else on board the ship was normal according to Captain Doane.

Yet, if Nickerson was guilty how could one man have overpowered three men to take command of the ship? And what was his motive for such actions? Regardless, Nickerson was formally charged with murder and piracy, to which he pleaded innocent. A trial was scheduled for July 1773, during which the prosecution could not prove beyond a reasonable doubt that Nickerson had performed the accused deeds. Adams' defense of Nickerson maintained that the Chatham man was a lucky survivor of a pirate attack on the high seas, and that he was not in any way involved. After two hours of deliberation the judges returned with a four-to-four vote, and therefore, under the rules of the court, a "not guilty" verdict for the defendant. He was cleared of all charges and freed. Despite the acquittal, the people of Boston, and of Cape Cod, were not certain of exactly what had happened aboard the *Abigail* on that November night.

Indeed, even Adams was left confused by the whole *Abigail* ordeal. After the trial was concluded he wrote in his diary, "This was and remains still a mysterious transaction. I know not to this day what judgment to form of his guilt or innocence." Years later he wrote, "I suppose the want of direct evidence afforded room for doubt in the minds of the majority."

For years afterwards, conflicting accounts continued to envelop the case in a shroud of confusion. Some retellings of the tale indicate that Captain Doane witnessed bloodstained decks on the *Abigail* and saw the bodies of the two Nickerson men and Newcomb. Other accounts clearly indicate that Doane witnessed no bodies and no blood at all. Some accounts mention a British ship while other accounts suggest French pirates. It has been said that Nickerson was put on trial two times, each time found not guilty.

Interestingly, Ansel Nickerson was married exactly one year to the day before the *Abigail* affair, on November 14, 1771 to Mary Smith of Chatham. His exploits later in life remain rather cloudy. Most accounts show Nickerson living another decade and a half and even fighting for the cause of independence during the Revolutionary War. His death, in the West Indies, is an additional source of controversy. One story reveals that he was convicted of murder on Saint Eustatius, in the Netherlands Antilles, where he was put to death by hanging. Another tale indicates that Nickerson died in Martinique, where he confessed to the murders on board the *Abigail*. Either way, it remains one of Cape Cod's more bizarre mysteries.

Stories from Prohibition Days

In the 1920s the country went dry. With the 18th Amendment, the sale and production of liquor was outlawed. Citizens had to figure out how to live with the so-called "noble experiment." Many decided they didn't like the idea. Entrepreneurs quickly seized upon the opportunity to supply a prohibited item to a consuming public that seemed to delight in flaunting the law. Rumrunning became big business along the New England coast and Cape Cod was perfectly situated to intercept the clandestine cargoes of booze. The Cape and Islands became a prime bootlegging territory.

The twelve-mile offshore line was the end of Coast Guard jurisdiction and bootleggers offered their supplies of bourbon, rye, champagne, scotch, and cognac to passing vessels with impunity. With the Coast Guard stretched out over a large coastal patrol area, skillful captains could bring a cargo into a deserted cove and deliver it to waiting trucks. Each Cape community had individuals that were involved in liquor smuggling. The profits were huge and a man could make as much as $400 a month in the illegal liquor trade.

Perhaps the most celebrated rumrunner from the Cape was captain Manny Zora of Provincetown. Zora, a Portuguese fisherman, was

known as "The Sea Fox" because of his ability to slip through the
Coast Guard patrols in his fishing vessel, the *Mary Ellen*. In the dark
of night or under the shroud of a spring fog, this colorful rogue delivered cases of contraband to thirsty consumers all along the length
of Cape Cod. He became something of a folk hero to the Portuguese
community at the Cape-tip and his exploits were recounted for years
after he quit the trade, reportedly as a wealthy man, retiring to spend
his last days in his native Portugal.

It wasn't difficult to obtain liquor during the height of Prohibition.
Most towns featured "tea rooms" and "speak easies" where a person
could get a drink and locals winked at the activities that went on in them.
Otherwise respectable citizens took the opportunity to profit from the
liquor trade whenever possible. The lighthouse keeper in Chatham was
caught hiding a stash of bootleg whiskey in the fog horn building. One
Brewster selectman is reported to have made it a practice to store his
water-dropped whiskey in a fish weir off Robbins Hill Beach.

With potential profits so high, organized crime was naturally
attracted to the bootlegging business. While most rumrunning encounters with the authorities, or even with hijackers, ended with
perhaps a few bruised knuckles, a small fine, or the loss of the cargo,
rumrunning could turn deadly.

In 1923, the Newport, Rhode Island-based rumrunner *John Dwight*
was apparently caught in a "turf war" over who had the rights to
run booze into Martha's Vineyard. In a deadly shootout, the *Dwight*
was apparently sunk by a competitor and its crew of nine men was
tortured and set adrift to die in the cold April sea. With no witnesses,
it could only be surmised that the fate of the *Dwight* crew resulted
because someone wanted to send a strong message that competitors
were not welcome in Vineyard Sound.

But there was humor in the story of rumrunning as well. In December of 1922, the Canadian rumrunner *Annie Spindler* was driven
by the winds of a northeaster onto the Provincetown beach near the
Race Point Coast Guard station. She had sailed from Nova Scotia
with a large cargo of whiskey and it was pretty certain that if the
unfortunate storm did not leave her on the sand, the *Spindler* would
have sold her cargo from the safety of her Rum Row anchorage.

By a strange twist of fate, the Coast Guard was obligated to assist

Rumrunner Annie Spindler *ashore at Provincetown, 1922.*
Source: H.A. Dickerman & Son, Taunton, Massachusetts. Jim Coogan collection

the captain in bringing his cargo of booze from the wrecked ship to another vessel that was tied up in Provincetown Harbor. As a foreign vessel, the *Spindler* and her cargo were eligible for protection because she carried papers indicating that her destination was the West Indies. The Coast Guard, faced with a simple act of God, had no choice but to assist in the transfer of the liquor. This was done, although at a considerable loss of much of the cargo at the hands of willing local "volunteers" who made off with a good deal of the merchandise. What was left was loaded onto a second vessel and shortly after departing Provincetown the remainder of the booze was delivered ashore at a secluded cove further up Cape.

Smugglers were also creative. There was a report that a former German navy submarine was operating off the Cape and Islands and shooting booze-filled torpedoes toward the shore for pick-up. But not every liquor drop was successful. One night a rumrunner was being chased by a Coast Guard cutter near Billingsgate Shoal. The captain decided to drop his cargo overboard in shallow water, marking his position so as to be able to return later to pick it up. It didn't take long for word of the drop to spread through the local community and the next morning, to the bootlegger's dismay he found that several hundred Cape Codders were already in position dragging the bottom for the jettisoned whiskey. There wasn't much left for him to salvage.

Although it hasn't happened recently, an occasional bottle of bootleg whiskey might still appear in the shifting tidal flats of Cape Cod Bay. In the early 1960s a Brewster sea clammer stumbled on several bottles still with the corks in them. He reported that the taste of the booze wasn't compromised a bit by its lengthy sleep in the sand.

Captain Josiah Knowles and the Saga of the Wild Wave

On February 9, 1858, Captain Josiah Knowles departed San Francisco for New York in the 1,500-ton clipper ship *Wild Wave*. Save for the loss of a crewman over the side in the first week of the voyage, the trip south toward the Horn was uneventful. The ship was logging extended periods of 10 to 13-knot speeds and the 27-year old Brewster skipper was confident that his ship would arrive in New York sometime in May. He had no idea that circumstances were about to force him to embark on one of the great sea adventures of the century.

It was late in the evening on March 5, as the clipper moved south on her track in the vicinity of 24 degrees south latitude and 130 degrees east longitude, when the captain was awakened in his cabin by the shout of one of the ship's lookouts, "Breakers under the lee!" This seemed impossible. Charts indicated that the *Wild Wave* was nowhere near land. Yet as Captain Knowles came up on deck, he could see a line of breakers dead ahead. Even as he gave the command to put the ship's wheel hard over, it was clear to him that there would be no escape for the *Wild Wave*. She slammed into a coral reef at great speed causing her masts to snap forward. In the confusion, Captain Knowles rallied his men to action. Fortunately, the ship had wedged herself so solidly into the reef that there was no immediate danger that she might sink, but a large and visible hole in the hull made it immediately clear that the *Wild Wave* had reached her final resting place.

In the morning, Captain Knowles took stock of his situation. His 30-man crew and ten passengers were amazingly unharmed and the sea had subsided enough so that the ship's boats could be put over the side. The captain ordered several crewmembers to row into the nearby lagoon and survey the small atoll which lay before them. It proved to be Oeno Island, a small, uninhabited piece of ground, not much more than a sandbar covered with palm trees. For some reason, navigation charts had incorrectly placed the island about 20 miles to the west. Reliance on this faulty chart had proved fatal to the *Wild Wave*.

Captain Knowles got his crew and passengers off in the boats and they settled ashore in tents made from salvaged sail canvas. A walk around the two-mile long spit revealed that there was some fresh water and enough birds, fish, and clams for survival. But, the real question in the minds of all of the survivors was whether anyone would ever look for them in this remote corner of the Pacific Ocean.

Oeno Island, despite its ability to sustain the castaways, proved to be what Captain Knowles described as "a dreary waste of sand." Tropical heat burned the survivors of the *Wild Wave* by day. At night the survivors were bedeviled by aggressive land crabs and, an army of rats that apparently had reached the island from an earlier shipwreck. After a week of burning signal fires and not seeing any passing ships, Captain Knowles suggested a bold plan. He estimated that Pitcairn Island was about eighty miles to the south of Oeno. He proposed taking one of the ship's boats, with a few volunteers, and try and reach that British possession to gain assistance. On March 13, Captain Knowles, his first mate, and five crewmen departed Oeno for the voyage to Pitcairn Island.

It took just two days to reach Pitcairn but the island was strangely quiet. Notices on trees showed that two years earlier the islanders had been evacuated by the British government to Norfolk Island. Pitcairn was silent and abandoned.

At least food was not a problem. Chickens and goats – even a few cattle – apparently left behind when the inhabitants had been removed, provided a solid diet of meat. There were also vegetables and fruit trees and abundant sources of fresh water. But, as Captain Knowles ruefully acknowledged, there was little reason for any ships to call at this remote place and he and his crew were left in a relatively comfortable but potentially permanent island prison. To compound their situation, their small boat was pounded to pieces in a heavy surf.

Captain Knowles decided that their only hope of rescue was to build a boat and sail to Tahiti, some 1,500 miles away. But the men had few tools and no seasoned lumber. Any boat would have to be built from scratch and with whatever tools they could salvage from the abandoned island houses. The men set about their task, hacking and shaping tree trunks into planks with hand axes. Burning several houses gave them a supply of nails and they salvaged pieces of cloth and canvas found within the abandoned dwellings for sails.

It took almost two months for the boat to be finished. Named the *John Adams* after one of the first settlers of Pitcairn Island, she was about 30 feet in length and was schooner rigged. The mainmast came from the flagpole that had overlooked the abandoned settlement. With three of the crewmembers deciding to stay on Pitcairn, the others put to sea on July 23rd. They had been marooned on Pitcairn almost three months. Contrary winds caused Captain Knowles to alter his course away from Tahiti and toward the Marquesas. Navigating by the stars, the captain estimated that they were making about 100 miles a day. After almost two weeks at sea, they arrived at Nukahiva in the Marquesas.

Their landfall was fortunately timed. As they rounded the point that shielded the lagoon at Nukahiva they were astonished to find the American warship *USS Vandalia* at anchor there. She had arrived just one day before and was already making ready to leave for Tahiti. The *Vandalia* was the first ship that the survivors had seen in the almost six months since they had departed from San Francisco.

The crew of the *Vandalia* made the survivors welcome and marveled at their story. The warship headed to Tahiti where Captain Knowles recovered his strength and eventually was able to get back to San Francisco aboard a French ship. From there he made the trip back to the East Coast aboard the steamer *Golden Gate*, arriving in New York in late October. Even though his family had been alerted about his rescue, when Captain Knowles walked into his Brewster house on November 1st it was to his relatives as if someone had returned from the dead. And indeed, that might almost have described what Captain Knowles had done.

The *USS Vandalia* eventually sailed from Tahiti to Oeno and picked up the *Wild Wave's* remaining survivors. Though the conditions had been harsh, incredibly, only one man had died in the interim. The three men who had chosen to stay behind on Pitcairn Island were also rescued by the *Vandalia*, completing the incredible tale of voyage and rescue that had started on a dark night some six months earlier with the cry, "Breakers under the lee!"

Captain Knowles was carrying two things of importance aboard the *Wild Wave*. One was $18,000 in gold that he had been charged with transferring back to New York. The second was a personal item, the body of his brother, Thomas, who had died and had been buried in San Francisco in 1852. Captain Knowles had temporarily re-buried his brother's casket on Oeno after the wreck. When the *Vandalia* went to Oeno to pick up the castaways, Thomas Knowles' body was retrieved. Taken to San Francisco, it was eventually shipped back to Cape Cod for burial. As for the gold, it, too, arrived safely back on the East Coast in a container that, in all the six months of travail at sea, had never left the sight of Captain Josiah Knowles.

Oh, for a Cot in the Wilderness

Not all those who went to sea were thrilled with their oceangoing occupation. Even some of the saltiest mariners wanted nothing more than to get back home, to a safe harbor and the comfort of family and friends.

It is true that Cape Cod lads went to sea early, by age 15 or 16. They grew up before the mast, nearly all they learned as they passed through the portal from boyhood to manhood they learned upon the ocean waves. By the time they were twenty years old they had been to the ports of Europe and Asia, and had traveled down one side of South America and up the other. As others headed west via covered wagon, Cape Cod men headed west via Cape Horn. From the shores of this peninsula they journeyed far and wide to see a world most Americans had never imagined

Cape sailors moved up the ranks over their years at sea, perhaps becoming first mate or even master of a vessel. When one considers the long list of Cape Cod sea captains, the name Joshua Sears tends to appear near the top. Perhaps it's because he led such a long and successful career upon the world's oceans, revered by all that knew him or sailed with him. Perhaps it's because of the memorable ships he mastered, including the pride of the Shiverick clippers – the *Wild Hunter* – pushing each vessel to her limit. Perhaps it's simply because he represented the quintessential sea captain with his long white beard hiding a weathered face. Or perhaps, given all of the above, it is because through his ship logs and letters he showed a human side not normally associated with a hardened sea captain. His writings tell of his inner thoughts, providing readers with a deep glimpse of life on the high seas.

At the age of twenty Sears was a crewman of the *Eben Preble*, commanded by Captain James Crocker, on a one-year voyage to China to pick up a cargo of tea. Within three years he rose to the rank of first mate of the *Preble*. Seven years later he became master of the *Burmah* and with his first command he established his reputation as a "driver" by pushing his vessel and crew to produce speedy passages. During his many years at sea he outraced typhoons and pirates, and battled cholera and bouts of depression.

Captain Sears' next command was the *Orissa*, which he sailed a number of times to Calcutta from 1849 to 1854, his wife, Minerva, and daughter, Louise, accompanying him. But his most perfect fit with a vessel was his years as master of the clipper *Wild Hunter* on which he made his final voyage from 1857 to 1860. From Boston he made San Francisco four months later, and then took the vessel across the Pacific for Singapore. Over the next three years he acquired cargoes where he could find them in an attempt to put together a profitable voyage.

Here are excerpts from Captain Sears' log that give some indication of the inner thoughts of one of the Cape's foremost 19th century sea captains, revealing a captain who had fallen out of love with the sea.

September 5, 1857: "That heavy swell keeps running from the west. Patience, patience – Put your trust in God."

September 6: "Slow getting going – Thy ways, O Lord, are inscrutable."

September 9: "The Lord is my Shepherd; He'll guide me safe through"

September 13: "O for a Cot in some Wilderness."

September 25: "Dead calm all this day; Current set the Ship 20 miles due East. I never had such hard luck before."

September 26: "Oh how disconsolate I do feel. Next voyage I will go down the China Sea and face all the Typhoons that blows."

In March 1858 he longed for home, far away from the China Sea. On March 10 he wrote: "Oh for a home in some vast wilderness, where the waves of the ocean will trouble me no more." His homesickness had not improved a year later when, in April 1859, he wrote: "Sometimes

Clipper Ship Swallow *at Hong Kong. Courtesy of Jane Baxter*

I feel as if I wanted to jump overboard, but now I have a great desire to live and see my home again."

In December 1859 he fell ill, as reported in this letter home: "Four weeks ago ... I was taken with a sort of cholera so bad I thought I should hardly live through the night and I have not seen a well day since ... I think that I have got on the other side of the Hill and am sliding down, and when a person gets going, they are apt to go pretty fast ... I have never seen the need of a wife before so much as I have this voyage. But it will certainly take six months to get me tame enough to live with one ..." He goes on to write: "Sometimes I get very homesick and think I cannot hardly stand it; and at other times it seems as if I did not care whether I ever see home again or not."

By January 1860 he had finally secured enough cargo to head for home. Off the coast of South America on July 19, racing toward New York and the end of his seafaring career, Captain Sears wrote: "If ever one poor fellow was tired of anything, it is I, Josh Sears, that is sick and tired of going to sea." Arriving back on Cape Cod in autumn of 1860, he retired. His sailing days done, he spent his remaining twenty-five years with family and friends on dry land.

A Whale, a Tale and the 1893 Chicago Fair

There was a lot of excitement in the spring of 1892 when Captain Amos Chapman arrived in Provincetown. The captain had an ambitious plan to capture a live whale and exhibit the creature at the Chicago Columbian Exposition which was scheduled for the next year. Captain Chapman had come to the right place as Provincetown in the last years of the 19th century was the second most important whaling port in the United States after New Bedford. His plan was to bring a whale back to the Cape tip where it would be kept alive offshore over the winter in a double netted weir trap. Chapman's intention was to later bring the whale over to Chicago via the St. Lawrence Seaway where it would be put on display in a specially built tank.

Coming not that long after the success of Herman Melville's 1851 publication of *Moby Dick*, Captain Chapman was convinced that he had a sure thing. The public was eager to get a close-up look at these huge sea creatures. P.T. Barnum's display of a dead whale in New York City in the 1850s had brought crowds of thousands willing to pay to view it. The prospect of seeing a live leviathan in the Midwest was something that had the potential to make a lot of money.

Joining up with local whaler Captain John Dunham, master of the schooner *William A. Grozier*, Chapman and his crew spent the summer of 1892 on the Atlantic whaling grounds. Unfortunately for Captain Chapman, whales proved elusive and he returned to Provincetown in September empty handed. The chance of success slipped away as winter set in and the great plan came to nothing. The 1893 Chicago Fair opened on May 1, 1893. It featured the first hamburger, the "hootchy kootchy" dance of a belly dancer named "Little Egypt," Cracker Jacks, a Ferris wheel, and a "clasp locker" made for clothing, which was the forerunner to the zipper. But there was no live whale on display because Captain Chapman couldn't find one.

Chapter 4

Shipwrecks

The sands of Cape Cod mingle with the bones of lost vessels, a vast graveyard marking watery events which landlubbers can only imagine, and which Cape Cod mariners of the past knew only too well. One need only wander through the Cape's many cemeteries to view headstones calling out across the centuries with the telltale words "Lost at Sea" etched in slate to have some inkling of the woe that came to these shores for thousands of ships and hundreds of shipmates, and the widows they left behind.

The Girl Named For a Shipwreck

In January of 1857, the full-rigged 650-ton ship *Orissa*, captained by Cyrus Sears of Yarmouth, was driven up on Nauset Beach during a winter storm. The ship was bound for Boston from Calcutta with a cargo of gunny cloth and linseed. The particular winter season had been one of the worst in memory and many ships had been lost. Harbors were iced over and newspapers recorded eighteen-foot snowdrifts across Cape Cod. In the middle of this terrible season the *Orissa* became a casualty of the Atlantic beach.

Eastham's Captain Dean Gray Linnell headed the volunteer surf and rescue team that came to the aid of the stricken vessel. Three crewmembers and the first mate of the *Orissa* were lost as the ship wallowed in the surf. When the survivors were eventually taken off the hulk, Captain Linnell brought Captain Sears to his home to warm

(Above and opposite) Two headstones that point to four Cape mariners (three being brothers) all lost in the same storm – the October Gale of 1841. Photos: Adriana Sheedy.

up. Only ten days earlier, Captain Linnell and his wife, Mehitable, had welcomed a baby girl into their family – their seventh child. The baby still did not have a name and Captain Sears suggested that she be given the name of his ship. Thus the girl became Orissa Sears Linnell.

In gratitude for the rescue of himself and his crew, Captain Sears made a practice of regularly remembering little Orissa with gifts throughout her lifetime. Sadly, she became blind from a severe childhood illness and she died at a young age. It is one of the more curious facts of Cape Cod that with the many shipwrecks along the treacherous coastline, only one became the occasion of the name of a person – Orissa Sears Linnell.

Wreck of the Steamer Portland

Saturday, November 26, 1898 began peaceful enough, in no way suggesting the doom that was to come over the hours and days to follow. During the course of the day the seas grew with an increasing north wind. Around mid-afternoon, New York was reporting heavy snows and high winds. By nightfall, prudent sea captains were heading for safe harbor. Meanwhile, at Boston's India Wharf, more than 175 Thanksgiving passengers and crew boarded the steamer *Portland* for an overnight one hundred-mile voyage home after the holiday. By morning, they expected to be docking at the vessel's namesake Maine city.

Built in 1890 by the New England Shipbuilding Company of Bath, Maine, the *Portland* was a 291-foot long, 2,280-ton paddle wheel steamer. Along with her sister ship, *Bay State*, the two vessels made the daily run between Boston and Portland. The *Portland* had a maximum speed of fifteen knots. Her master was fifty-five-year-old Captain Hollis Henry Blanchard who was known as being very cautious. Even as the *Portland* left Boston Harbor at 7:00 p.m. the seas were mounting and the winds were becoming fierce. Ships of all kind passed the beautiful paddle wheel steamer as they headed in to batten down the hatches against the increasing nor'easter. It is impossible to understand why Captain Blanchard did not turn his vessel around and head back to India Wharf, unless he was under management orders to proceed.

The storm that would become known as the "Portland Gale" is believed to have been two storms that collided over southeastern New England. One storm was coming from the south. The captain and owners of the *Portland* were aware of this storm and must have figured that their vessel could outrun it on her way north to her homeport. This thinking is confirmed by the fact that the *Bay State*, scheduled to make the trip south from Portland to Boston that same evening, remained safely at her Portland, Maine berth rather than heading south into the storm. The Portland Steam Packet Company, though, was apparently unaware of a second storm with hurricane force winds coming down from the Great Lakes.

Around 9:00 p.m. the *Portland* was sighted off Gloucester, about three miles offshore. Another vessel witnessed her battling large waves near Thacher Island, off Gloucester. These ships were heading for port. Perhaps at this point Captain Blanchard was having second thoughts, but with the growing storm he knew he would risk capsizing his vessel by turning her around in such heavy seas. History, of course, tells that he should have taken the risk, yet Blanchard keep the *Portland's* bow pointed toward the onslaught.

By 11:00 p.m. the two storms converged, the snows became very heavy, and the winds shifted from north to northeast, reaching about 40 miles per hour and growing steadily throughout the night until reaching 70 miles per hour around 3:00 a.m. Ninety-mile-per-hour winds were measured at Nantucket. A tempest was unleashed, pounding the Cape and her waters with a force only rivaled by that of the great October Gale of 1841.

The *Portland* was still off Gloucester at 11:00 p.m., unable to make forward progress, yet continuing to battle the waves simply to survive. No doubt, at this point Captain Blanchard was merely attempting to outlast the storm. Around midnight, it is believed, the *Portland* was off Eastern Point Light, near Norman's Woe, perhaps attempting to reach Gloucester Harbor. She had been at sea for five hours and had only traveled thirty miles. Winds reached 60 miles per hour at that hour and still the storm had not reached its height. That would not occur until around 5:00 a.m., and it is believed that the *Portland* survived to that hour, or perhaps even later.

At daybreak, the ground was covered with a foot of snow, blocking railroad lines and in some areas the storm surge washing the rails away completely. Telegraph lines were down as Cape Cod found herself cut off from the rest of the world. Meanwhile, on the raging seas hundreds of vessels and thousands of mariners battled for their lives.

The next morning, November 28, wreckage and bodies from the

Portland began washing up along Outer Cape beaches from Truro to Chatham. The ship, her passengers, and her crew were lost somewhere in Massachusetts Bay between the Cape tip and Gloucester. By Tuesday morning the storm was over. In her terrible wake nearly two hundred vessels were sunk, with the loss of some five hundred souls, somewhere between 175 and 190 aboard the *Portland* alone (an exact number is not known).

With telegraph lines down, the country learned of the *Portland* disaster via France; news was cabled from Cape Cod across the Atlantic where it was relayed back to New York via Ireland and Newfoundland. The sheer magnitude of the destruction became clearer with each piece of twisted wreckage and with each frozen body found along the coastline. While on land, the damage was without precedent – ice-laden trees uprooted all over the Cape, homes and buildings damaged, streets flooded, and rail service disrupted. Normal life ground to a halt as Cape Codders dug out and then began to piece their lives back together. The storm would be named for its biggest prize as Cape Codders would refer to the "Portland Gale" for decades to come, comparing every storm thereafter with the "hundred year storm" of 1898.

The wreck of the *Portland* was eventually discovered ninety years after she went down, well north of Provincetown in the northern section of Stellwagen Bank National Marine Sanctuary off Gloucester. The once-beautiful vessel is now in a demolished state, sitting upright in water more than 70 fathoms deep, protected under the stipulations of the marine sanctuary.

Meanwhile, centuries later, memories of the storm and of the steamer that share the name *Portland* have forever become a part of Cape Cod and Massachusetts history and lore.

Dangerous Cargo

Sometimes, even after a ship has sunk it can still make its presence known. Such was the case with the steamer *Longfellow* upon one particular fall evening more than a century ago.

On September 9, 1904, the 413-ton steamer *Longfellow*, built in the 1870s and named to honor the famous poet of "Paul Revere's Ride" and "The Wreck of the Hesperus," was hauling a dangerous cargo up the backside of the Cape. At one time an excursion vessel, now converted to transport cargo, in her holds were some three hundred tons of dynamite en route to Portsmouth, New Hampshire. Unfortunately she would never make it as she ran into a nor'easter off Orleans and began to take on water.

Off Highland Light she was rolling in the heavy seas and the crew feared her shifting cargo might explode. They scrambled into two lifeboats and rowed away from the powder keg toward the glow of Coston flares held by surfmen on the beach from Pamet River, High Head, and Highland lifesaving stations. Sixteen crewmen from the *Longfellow* were brought ashore. There were no casualties and by the next morning life along the Outer Cape coast returned to normal. In time, the sunken *Longfellow* was forgotten.

September became October and then November. On the night of November 13th a gale swept the seas off Highland Light into a boil and the turbulence awakened the *Longfellow* from her two-month slumber, apparently slamming her sunken hull and her temperamental cargo against the ocean floor for two sizable explosions were felt across the Lower Cape within a fifteen-minute period. The cause of the ruckus was discovered over the days that followed as a large number of dead fish washed up along the beaches with mangled wreckage from the steamer *Longfellow*.

The Blueberry Shipwreck

On January 27, 1939, the British steam freighter *Lutzen* left Halifax, Nova Scotia on a routine trip to New York City. There was a high sea running and constant fog. Several days out, as the ship approached Cape Cod, Captain Robert Randall, the *Lutzen's* master, was essentially navigating in the blind.

Near midnight on February 2nd, Coast Guardsman Ed Dorion from the Orleans Life Saving Station was making his patrol along Nauset Beach. Out of the fog, he was startled to see a ship's running lights just about on top of him. Immediately he fired a warning flare just as the *Lutzen* struck a sandbar about 75 yards offshore. As the ship grounded, Dorion ran for help. Aboard the stricken vessel, Captain Randall wasn't sure where he was. He ordered the ship's lifeboat to be launched so two crewmen could row ashore to see if whoever fired the flare might be able to assist them. But there were heavy swells and the small boat was smashed against the *Lutzen's* hull, hurling both men into the cold sea. One was able to grab a line, but the other man was lost.

By morning, Coast Guardsmen from the Orleans and Old Harbor Station in Chatham had gathered, eventually taking the rest of the *Lutzen's* crew off the ship by surfboat. At this point authorities were faced with figuring a way to get the vessel off the beach. Some of the cargo had been tossed overboard to lighten the ship, but even with a couple of deep ocean tugs pulling, the *Lutzen* wouldn't budge. The bulk of the ship's cargo consisted of 250 tons of frozen blueberries. When it became clear that the *Lutzen* wasn't going anywhere, an attempt was made to offload the frozen fruit. Without refrigeration the berries would spoil. Fifty men were paid 75 cents an hour to pile the boxes of blueberries on shore in a roped and guarded area. But even as the berries were transported off the beach to waiting trucks, considerable pilfering took place. Many of the Coast Guardsmen were related to the scavengers and looked the other way as the blueberries disappeared. Four days after beaching, the *Lutzen* rolled over on her beam-ends, a total loss.

As for the stolen blueberries, they were initially very popular as Cape Codders from Orleans to Yarmouth made pancakes, muffins, jam, cookies – even ice cream. But after a month or so, the steady offerings of the salvaged fruit grew pretty tiresome. For months afterward a person visiting people on the Lower Cape could be greeted with a nasty look if they asked, "Got any blueberry pie?"

Sarcophagus of Steel

December 17, 1927 was a Saturday and the people of Provincetown went about their business as usual. Meanwhile, off the coast the crew of the Navy submarine S-4 out of Portsmouth, New Hampshire was testing their vessel after work performed on the sub at the Charlestown Navy Yard. The morning's exercises consisted of a series of dives in the more than one hundred-foot waters and all appeared to be working in fine order. At Wood End Coast Guard Station, Boatswain Emanuel Gracie watched the goings on with interest as he went about his duties.

Across Cape Cod Bay from Boston steamed the Coast Guard Cutter *Paulding*. The four-stack *Paulding* was a former World War I Navy destroyer now patrolling domestic waters in search of rumrunners. Her travels brought her to the Cape tip at precisely 3:37 p.m., making her way past Wood End Coast Guard Station at sixteen knots, and headed toward Provincetown Harbor. Neither her crew nor her master, Captain John S. Baylis, knew that below them was the submarine *S-4*. Below, the crew of *S-4* was equally unaware of the cutter's presence. Only Boatswain Gracie at the Wood End Station was aware of the tragedy unfolding before his very eyes.

The submarine broke the surface, colliding with the *Paulding's* bow, which sliced a hole in her hull just forward of the conning tower. Captain Baylis of the *Paulding* knew instantly what happened as it was known that the area was used as a testing ground for Navy submarines. He immediately sent a distress message that the cutter had collided with an unknown submarine off Wood End Light.

Meanwhile, beneath the surface, the crew of *S-4* had no chance of escape. The submarine sank in five minutes, coming to rest 110 feet below on the ocean floor. The *Paulding* lowered her boats, but detecting no survivors from the mortally wounded sub she limped toward Provincetown Harbor. As the *Paulding* made for the harbor, Boatswain Gracie of Wood End Station rowed out to the area where the collision occurred and lowered his grapnel line in hopes of snagging the sub. For six hours in the most unpleasant winter conditions, much of it in darkness, Gracie dragged the waters in search of the wrecked submarine. Finally he found her only to have gale force winds snap his line. Exhausted and cold, he abandoned the search until morning.

When he awoke the next morning he found that rescue operations were still not underway although the *Falcon*, a salvage vessel, had arrived at Provincetown Harbor. *S-4's* mother ship, *Bushnell*, was on her way from Portsmouth. Wooden pontoons were being towed from New York and divers were being brought in from Newport, Rhode Island. The Secretary of the Navy, the Chief of Navy Operations, and a number of admirals were all on their way to Provincetown to investigate the incident and to oversee rescue operations.

Gracie returned to the scene of the collision and was successful in once again locating the submarine with his grapnel line. The *Falcon*

In the cemetery at the Congregational Church, on Truro's Hill of Churches, rests this enclosed monument that reads, "Sacred to the memory of 57 citizens of Truro who were lost in seven vessels which foundered at sea in the memorable gale of Oct 3, 1841." The storm also took the lives of other Cape Cod mariners, including more than 20 from Dennis. Photo: Jack Sheedy

came alongside and, with Gracie's line, was now connected to the sunken submarine below. Unfortunately, high seas made it almost impossible to dive to the wreck that morning so the crew of the *Falcon* and the divers who arrived from Newport waited for the winds to let up. Eventually they realized that somebody had to risk a dive to see if anyone was alive below. That person would be Tom Eadie. He donned his diving suit and went over the side to follow the grapnel line to the submarine. At the depth of more than one hundred feet, and with the waves churning everything up, visibility was only a few feet at best. As his feet made contact with the hull he immediately heard tapping from inside. With a hammer, Eadie tapped international Morse code on the hull to discover that six crewmen had survived the collision in the forward torpedo room.

Eadie returning to the surface. It was now Bill Carr's turn to dive to *S-4* and attach an air hose to the ballast tank connection in order to bring the submarine to the surface. Valves were turned and air rushed through the hose to the damaged vessel below, yet the damage proved to be more severe than the rescuers first guessed as air bubbles began to appear on the surface foretelling of a leak in the ballast tank. As weather conditions deteriorated it was decided that one last dive would be attempted to bring a hose below to pump fresh air into the torpedo room and thus keep the men alive until a rescue effort could be employed with the use of the pontoons coming from New York.

Fred Michaels donned his gear and then down he went with the air hose to land atop the sub. But the rocking of the ship above, and the impact on his lifeline, caused him to slip off the sub to become embedded in the ocean floor mud. With help from the crew on the rescue vessel above, who carefully pulled on his lifeline, Michaels was freed from the mud, but then got ensnared in the S-4's wreckage. He called above to alert them to his situation, necessitating another diver to go below to release Michaels. Eadie made his way below for a second time and was successful in untangling Michaels, who had been weakened by the ordeal. Thoughts of attaching the air hose to the submarine were dashed when Eadie tore his diving suit on a piece of the sharp wreckage and had to be returned to the surface.

Conditions on the following day were no better. It was still whipping a gale and rescue operations were put on hold until a break in the weather. By that evening, it was estimated, the air supply in the sub would be exhausted, yet weather conditions made diving on the submarine too risky. Finally, two mornings later the storm let up and preparations were made to dive only to discover that the buoy line to the submarine had disconnected. Upon hearing this news, the entire fishing fleet of Provincetown offered to sweep across the area with their draggers in order to locate the sub quickly so rescue operations could continue. Amazingly, the Navy declined the fishermen's offer as the *Falcon* groped blindly with a single drag line until S-4 was located later that day. A diver was lowered, an air hose was attached, and fresh air was pumped into the torpedo room. Alas, those who had survived the initial collision and subsequent sinking were now all dead. The rescue operation now became a salvage operation. When weather improved, divers went down to bring up the dead.

On March 17th, three months after the disaster, S-4 was raised and then towed to the Charlestown Navy Yard for repairs. She was later used as an experimental salvage vessel, particularly in the rescue of trapped crews underwater.

Cape Cod history will long remember the tale of six men sealed in a sarcophagus of steel on the ocean floor, and of the divers who attempted to free them.

CG 36500 & the Pendleton

A storm visited Cape Cod on the night of February 18, 1952, churning the waters off Chatham into a sea of gigantic waves. Upon that night two large tankers split in half, thus setting the stage for one of the Cape's most courageous rescue efforts.

The evening began with a distress call from the tanker *Fort Mercer*, which had broken in two in rough seas southwest of Chatham. Coast Guard cutters from a number of northeast stations headed for the waters off Cape Cod while a PBY Catalina out of Salem Naval Air Station flew over the turbulent waters. Of the *Fort Mercer's* crew, some were on the stern section while others remained on the severed bow. Coast Guard cutters *Acushnet, Yakatat,* and *Eastwind* swept in to pick up the survivors. During the rescue efforts, thirteen crewmen were lost.

Yet, another high seas drama was taking place fifty miles away off Monomoy where a second tanker, the *Pendleton*, was also drifting in two pieces. En route to Boston, the vessel broke up that morning off Provincetown, the damage to the ship knocking out the radio transmitter, preventing a distress call. While rescue efforts were being concentrated on the *Fort Mercer*, those at the Coast Guard station at Chatham were monitoring the two radar blips of the *Pendleton*. They rightly surmised that the blips belonged to another large ship that had split in half. A rescue had to be attempted and Chatham had the only crew available. Ordered to command the rescue boat was twenty-three year old Coxswain Bernie Webber. The events of that evening would include mountainous waves and seventy-mile-per-hour winds. Webber knew there was a good chance he would not return, and yet he had to select a crew to accompany him. Three of his station comrades – Andrew Fitzgerald, Richard Livesey, and Irving Maske – stepped forward to volunteer.

Coast Guard lifeboat CG 36500 *at Rock Harbor and in dry dock.*
Photos: Jack Sheedy

From Chatham fish pier, in the 36-foot motorized lifeboat *CG 36500*, the four men set off into seas higher than their vessel was long and against hurricane force winds. On the way out their boat was damaged by battering waves. The windshield was broken, the compass and rescue equipment were lost overboard, and the engine stalled a number of times. Without a compass or radar, the vessel picked its way over the crashing waves with the aid of those back at the Chatham station who monitored the positions of the *CG 36500* and the tanker on radar and then communicated the heading. Somehow, with everything against them, they were able to safely arrive at the stern section of the tanker *Pendleton*.

Upon the stern were all thirty-three surviving members of the tanker's crew. Next came the difficult task of transferring the men from the *Pendleton* to the lifeboat below. The Jacob's ladder was employed, allowing the crewmen to lower themselves over the side of the listing tanker. The *CG 36500* made two dozen passes, each time one or two crewmen from the *Pendleton* dropped to the lifeboat below. Occasionally, men missed the boat completely and fell into the ocean, yet the Coast Guardsmen plucked them free of the waves. Unfortunately, one tanker crewman was lost in the transfer.

With thirty-six men on a lifeboat with a maximum capacity of twenty-three, Webber motored away from the tanker's stern and headed landward for what all on board assumed would be an arduous journey toward safety. With the navigational equipment gone, the crew made a best guess as to where land might be and hoped to at least find the beaches of Monomoy Island where they could beach their boat. As the vessel battled waves on its way in Webber became concerned. They should have reached Monomoy by now, that is, if they were heading in the right direction. Suddenly, in the gloom they saw a flashing red light. As the lifeboat drew nearer they recognized it as a buoy – it was the buoy marking the entrance to Chatham Harbor. Remarkably, the *CG 36500* emerged from a raging sea to motor right up to the fish pier where the impossible rescue operation had commenced earlier that evening.

The crew from the *Pendleton*, many of them injured, chilled to the bone, or in a state of shock, were assisted out of the lifeboat by a large crowd of Chatham residents who had gathered at the pier awaiting the safe return of *CG 36500*. Many of the tanker crew were praying and sobbing at their good fortune. The four Chatham Coast Guardsmen were later awarded the Gold Lifesaving Medal for their bravery, the Guard's highest honor.

As for the *CG 36500*, she was decommissioned in 1968 and, because she was a Gold Lifesaving Medal boat, was given to the Cape Cod National Seashore. She was later presented to the Orleans Historical Society and restored by a dedicated group of volunteers, many of whom were retired Coast Guardsmen. The renovated vessel is on display at Rock Harbor during the summer season.

The Atlantic Ocean off the Outer Cape coastline is like a great book filled with stories of shipwrecks and of lifesavers. Earning a well-deserved chapter in that book are the events of the *Pendleton* rescue.

Remains of the German vessel Frances, *which wrecked in 1872 at Head of the Meadow Beach in Truro, as she appeared in 1999. Photo: Jack Sheedy*

Chapter 5

Lighthouses and Lifesavers

Today, lighthouses, though still serving an important nautical function, are largely seen as picturesque and majestic – something to snap a photo of while on vacation. Yet, their continued presence should remind us that despite our grand technological advances nature is still a force to respect and the sea at night can be unforgiving. At one time there were eighteen lighthouses positioned around the peninsula, eleven built along the forearm of the Cape along with thirteen lifesaving stations from Provincetown to Monomoy, their positioning dictated by the bulk of 19th century oceangoing traffic, and the lion share of shipwrecks.

Lighthouses of the Outer Cape Coast

Highland Light, also known as Cape Cod Light, is the site of the Cape's very first lighthouse. Built in 1797, she was the only beacon to meet mariners along their dark and dangerous journey from Nantucket to Boston. In 1808 her beam was joined by those of two wooden lighthouses built in the relative location of the present Chatham Light. Highland had fifteen lamps burning while each of the Chatham towers had but six. The Chatham twins were movable, therefore serving as range lights designed to mark the harbor entrance; by lining up the two lights as one approached a mariner was able to navigate safely through the channel.

By 1837, the stretch of darkness between Highland and Chatham was illuminated when three small brick lighthouses were constructed on

Two of the "Three Sisters" Lighthouses, which once stood on a cliff overlooking the Atlantic. Photo: Jack Sheedy

a cliff near the spot where the present Nauset Light now rises. Four years later, the two Chatham lighthouses tumbled over the eroding cliffs, so two new brick light towers with nine lamps each were built, later replaced with a 4th order Fresnel lens system.

Meanwhile, Highland Light was deemed unsafe and was completely rebuilt in 1857, receiving a 1st order Fresnel lens – the largest available at that time. During that same year the three lighthouses at Nauset were upgraded to include 6th order Fresnel lenses, which were upgraded fifteen years later to 4th order.

The year 1879 saw the southernmost tower of the second generation Chatham twins crumble over the side of the eroding cliff, which had lost more than two hundred feet in less than a ten-year period. Chatham operated with just one tower for two years until the cliff

The majestic view from atop Highland Light in Truro – the lighthouse was erected in 1857 and moved back from the cliff in the 1990s. Photos: Jack Sheedy

finally took the north tower to join its twin down below. To replace them, two iron-shelled lighthouses were installed further back from the cliff; the south tower is the present-day Chatham Light.

By 1892, the three brick lighthouses of Nauset fell in ruins down the cliff to the beach below. Three new, slightly taller wooden towers, which became known as the "Three Sisters" because from sea they looked like three women wearing smocks, were constructed atop the Nauset cliff. But it didn't take long for erosion to threaten these three newest beacons as well, so in 1918 the north and south light towers were sold to become part of an Eastham cottage. The middle "Sister" stood alone atop the dune until 1923 when she, too, was sold off to become part of another cottage in town. That same year, the northernmost Chatham twin was dismantled and moved north where it was reconstructed to become the present Nauset Light. It was painted red and white and was given alternating red and white beams to distinguish her from Highland Light to the north and Chatham Light to the south. In the 1990s, both Highland and Nauset lights were relocated back a ways from their eroding cliffs to save them from destruction, for the time being, that is, for erosion is ongoing, which will necessitate future moves.

And in 1990, the "Three Sisters" were reunited. Along Cable Road, just a few hundred yards west of the current Nauset Light, sit the trio of snug light towers, only the middle one still adorned with its lantern room. They reside in an opening in the woods, each one hundred and fifty feet apart, exactly as they once sat upon a cliff that has long since eroded away.

Women Lighthouse Keepers

The lantern room of Highland Lighthouse, built on the cliffs of Truro in 1857. Photo: Jack Sheedy.

For the most part, the lighthouse keepers were men, often retired seafarers who knew the value of a navigation beacon on a stormy night. But there were a few women who became full-time keepers in the nineteenth century and it does not seem that the safety of sailors at sea was in any way compromised by their unusual occupation.

Perhaps the earliest female lighthouse keeper on Cape Cod was Angeline Nickerson, who succeeded her husband, Simeon Nickerson, as full-time keeper of the Chatham twin lights from 1848 to 1859. Apparently, there was some initial grumbling by some of the citizens of the town and there was a movement to have her replaced by a man. But Mrs. Nickerson had her supporters and a number of them came to her defense. Resident Joshua Nickerson (undoubtedly a cousin) went so far as to write a letter to President Zachary Taylor endorsing Angeline in which he stated that, "she had discharged her duties ... in a most careful and faithful manner." The campaign to bring in a new male keeper at Chatham soon stopped.

Sandy Neck Light, which was situated at the bayside entrance to Barnstable Harbor, had two female lighthouse keepers. Lucy J. Baxter was in charge of this light between 1862 and 1867, succeeding her husband, F. T. Baxter. This was a period when the harbor was very active with vessels arriving from and traveling to all parts of the world. Records indicate that Eunice Crowell Howes, wife of Jacob Stone Howes, also ran the lighthouse for two years in the latter part of the nineteenth century.

*The current Chatham Lighthouse, which is the twin of Nauset Light to the north.
Photo: Jack Sheedy*

Another Cape woman, Sarah Cleverly Atwood of Wellfleet was appointed as keeper of the Mayo Beach Light in Wellfleet Harbor in 1876. She was the widow of William N. Atwood, a disabled Civil War veteran who had held the job since his return from the war. At his death it seemed clear that the most qualified person to carry on the duties of the light was his wife. She had assisted him for years to the point that she knew everything there was to know about the operation of the beacon.

Realizing that they had the perfect candidate for the job already living there, the government, in a rare demonstration of logic, turned the responsibilities over to Mrs. Atwood. She remained as keeper until 1891 when she resigned and moved "uptown" to East Commercial Street. "Aunt Sarah," as she was known to scores of Wellfleet youngsters, continued to be a fixture in the town until her death at the age of 83 on November 20, 1920.

The red and white tower of Nauset Light in Eastham, which casts an alternating red and white beam. Photo: Jack Sheedy.

Bishop and Clerks' Lighthouse

Just south of Great Island in West Yarmouth is a dangerous line of rocks that has long been a danger to mariners. Colonial records indicate that the area was once an island of almost five acres that for many years supported sheep grazing before the relentless tides and winter storms submerged the land sometime in the mid-eighteenth century.

Bishop and Clerks Lighthouse.
Source: Hugh C. Leighton Co. Portland, Maine.
Jim Coogan collection.

Left behind was a dangerous shoal and a series of eight large rocks, one very large that was nicknamed "the Bishop," and the rest, his "Clerks."

In the nineteenth century Nantucket Sound was a major shipping route and, with no Cape Cod Canal, large numbers of coasting vessels used this sea highway to transfer cargoes of lumber, coal, ice, and salt fish to New England ports.

In 1858, a solid stone lighthouse was built to mark the rocky ledge. The structure was almost seventy feet high and flashed a white light accompanied by a warning bell every thirty seconds. The wooden structure that was attached to the light tower housed the bell and fog horn.

Once the canal was completed, in 1914, it offered a shorter and safer route around Cape Cod. And as the maritime fortunes of New England declined in the first years of the twentieth century there was no longer a need to maintain the great number of navigation lights in Nantucket Sound. In 1928, the light was taken out of service and abandoned. After years of watching the structure disintegrate and fearing that its continued presence might attract the curious day-sailing adventurer, the Coast Guard dynamited the lighthouse in the fall of 1952. Today there is only a pyramid-shaped radar reflector on the site of the old tower to warn modern sailors of the still very real dangers of the waters around Bishop and Clerks' shoal.

USL SS to the Rescue

In the decades straddling the turn of the 20th century, in the years before the Cape Cod Canal was dug, and in a time when shipwrecks frequented the Outer Cape shore, a legion of surfmen patrolled the dark shores of night. For forty-three years this patrol guarded the Lower Cape beaches – forty-three years of winters, blizzards, hurricanes, and nor'easters – battling the shoals and bars of Race Point, Peaked Hill, Pamet River, Nauset, and Monomoy. For forty-three years shipwrecked sailors caught in the web of a watery grave were snatched up and cast safely upon the shore like Jonah spat from the belly of the whale.

The Old Harbor Life Saving Station, once a Chatham station, now resides at Race Point in Provincetown. Photo: Jack Sheedy

To trace the beginnings of the Life Saving Service of Cape Cod one must look to the Massachusetts Humane Society, formed in 1786 and considered the first in the country established to assist shipwreck survivors. The society built ninety-two small refuge huts along the coastline at locations prone to wrecks, providing victims fortunate enough to make it to shore with shelter and provisions until help could arrive. Although intentions were good, the plan failed as the stations were built too far apart and were manned by inexperienced volunteers.

In 1872, the government came up with a new plan, establishing the United States Life Saving Service (USLSS) and initially building nine stations on Cape Cod. This plan involved hiring a keeper and a team of paid surfmen to man each station, rather than volunteers. The keeper, who had to be a "man of good character" between the ages of twenty-one and forty-five, in good physical shape, and an expert boatman, lived at the station year round. Surfmen were hired on a year-to-year basis and were assigned from August 1 until June 1 of the following year. They worked six days a week with Sundays off. These surfmen were ranked according to their experience, with Number 1 being the highest rank – sort of like First Mate on a ship.

The stations were built between three and five miles apart; they were placed at Race Point, Peaked Hill Bars, Highlands, Pamet River, Cahoon's Hollow, Eastham, Orleans, Chatham, and on Monomoy. They were later joined by four other stations: High Head at Truro in 1883, Wood End at Provincetown in 1897, Old Harbor at Chatham in 1898, and at Monomoy Point in 1902. The typical layout of a three-story station included a kitchen, mess, keeper's room, and the boat and beach apparatus room on the lower level. Crew sleeping quarters and a storeroom, which doubled as a wreck survivors sleeping quarters, were located on the second level. And the third story held the observation tower. The boat and beach apparatus room normally housed two surfboats, a dory, and carriages to transport the boats to the wreck location. The room also held two sets of breeches buoy and carts to carry apparatus down to the beach.

A station's work week began at midnight on Sunday. Each day there was a different task. For instance, on Monday the crew might clean up around the station and made sure all equipment was in working

Surfmen readying a life boat for launching. Source: H.A. Dickerman & Son, Taunton, Massachusetts. Jim Coogan collection.

order. On Tuesday there might be lifeboat drills, Wednesday might be drilling in the use of international and general signal codes in order to communicate with passing ships, Thursday – breeches buoy drills, Friday – drilling in first aid, and Saturday was typically wash day.

And each night, regardless of weather conditions, surfmen walked the beach during watches which ran from sunset to 8:00 p.m., from 8:00 p.m. to midnight, from midnight to 4:00 a.m., and from 4:00 a.m. until sunrise. Starting out from their station, one surfman walked north and the other south for about two and a half miles until reaching a halfway hut or a designated ending point; there he would meet a surfman from the neighboring station with whom he might exchange information before each walked back to their respective station. The entire length of the Outer Cape, from Wood End to Monomoy Point, was monitored in this fashion throughout the night, from dusk till dawn.

Surfmen carried a Coston signal flare, which would be ignited to signal a wrecked ship that help was on the way. Then the station crew was mustered and depending upon the location of the wreck, and the weather conditions, a decision was made as to the best mode of rescue, whether via land or sea. For instance, if the wreck was well offshore a surfboat was launched. This was quite a feat, which required dragging a twenty-four foot long, one thousand-pound boat in a cart across miles of sand, down dune cliffs, in pitch darkness, and in wind, rain, or snow. The boat was then launched into the raging sea, along a coastline boasting fierce undertows, into a fury which had ensnared a two-hundred-foot vessel breaking up on the bars ahead. Crewmen could tumble into the sea and be lost, or a surfboat could become capsized, or be crushed by the bulk of the wrecked vessel lurching in the waves.

If the seas proved too rough to launch a boat, and the wreck was close enough to shore, the breeches buoy apparatus was employed, which created in a matter of minutes a pulley system between the ship and shore over which shipwreck victims could be transported. First, a Lyle gun, resembling a miniature cannon, was used to fire a shot into the rigging of the wrecked vessel. A crewman aboard retrieved the line carried by the shot, allowing ropes to be hauled over and fastened to a mast. Then the breeches buoy, so-called because it resembled a pair of canvas breeches with a buoyant tube at the waist, was hauled over to the ship to transport the crewmen to shore.

These methods proved successful, for during the USLSS' first decade, of the one hundred and seventy vessels wrecked along the Cape coast guarded by the Life Saving Service only about 20 of the roughly 1,200 people involved in these wrecks were lost. Meanwhile, the opening of the Cape Cod Canal in 1914 and the development of safer steel-hulled ships powered by propeller saw a dramatic reduction in the numbers of wrecks along the Outer Cape coastline. In 1915, the USLSS was merged with the Revenue Cutter Service to become the US Coast Guard.

The Monomoy Disaster

Cape Cod waters mark the final resting place for some three thousand shipwrecks. Unfortunately, most of these wrecks – and their stories – have become lost and forgotten within the mists of time. Yet, the story of the brave men who participated in the Monomoy Disaster will perhaps be forever remembered as more than a century later it still commands our attention, for contained within the morning of March 17, 1902 was a drama that transcends generations.

Adjacent to Chatham Light, upon a cliff overlooking the ocean, is a monument that relates the story of that fateful March day. Chiseled into stone are the names and the deeds that have since linked the name "Monomoy" with the word "disaster" so thoroughly for those who study the maritime history of this coastline and who recall the stories of those men who fought against its wrath despite the odds.

The monument reads: *"In memory of the hero of the Monomoy Disaster, Capt. Elmer F. Mayo, Chatham, MA, and his gallant rescue of Surfman Seth L. Ellis from a watery grave on Shovelful Shoals off Monomoy Point, March 17, 1902."*

Fourteen men were involved in the events of that March morning: twelve who perished and two who survived. Widows mourned, children become fatherless, Cape Codders held vigils, and the two survivors were hailed as heroes who put their lives in harm's way for the chance of saving the life of another.

Fog clung to the waves off Monomoy Island while offshore two barges, the *Wadena* and the *Fitzpatrick*, rested on Shovelful Shoals where they had stranded on March 11 after breaking away from the tug *Peter Smith*. Crews from both barges had earlier been taken ashore by the skilled surfmen of Captain Marshall Eldredge's Monomoy Life Saving Station. Wrecking crews were now on both vessels attempting to lighten their cargoes so they might be floated off the shoal, although most of the wreckers came ashore on the evening of March 16 due to bad weather and rough seas. The crew at the Monomoy Station assumed all the wreckers had left the barges, so they were surprised the next morning to see a distress signal flying above the *Wadena*. Though there was no sign of trouble, the code of the Life Saving Service was clear: "You must go out!" So out they went – Captain Eldredge and seven members of his crew.

Against the rough waters of a gale they rowed, and against rips considered the most treacherous along the Cape shoreline, and they were successful in reaching the *Wadena*. Captain Eldredge's crew pulled to the leeward side, took off the barge crew of five, and then headed for shore. That's when disaster struck. A large wave engulfed the surfboat; the lifesaving crew continued to row despite the swamped condition of the surfboat, following Captain Eldredge's orders to the letter according to the lone survivor. The wreckers, meanwhile, in a state of panic managed to capsize the boat. One by one, the men in

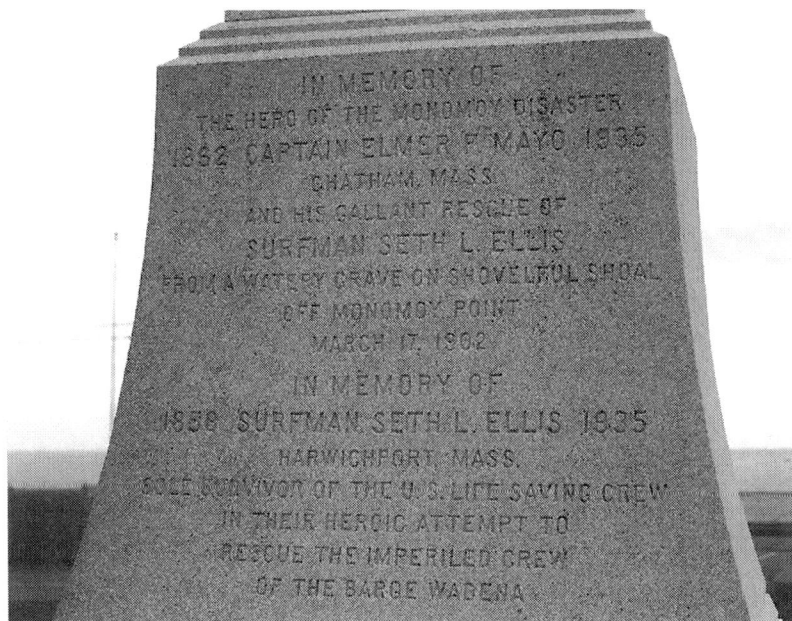

The "Mack" monument at Chatham – detailing the events and the participants in the Monomoy Disaster of 1902 – overlooking the waters of Shovelful Shoal in the background. Photo: Jack Sheedy.

the water drowned, first the five wreckers and then the lifesavers as they twice righted the surfboat in rough seas only to have it capsize for a third and final time. Only Number 1 Surfman Seth Ellis remained alive, clinging to the centerboard of the capsized boat. Fatigued, he could do nothing but hang on for as long as his strength would allow.

Seth Ellis was born in 1858, the son of a sea captain by the same name. At age nine he first went to sea, with his father, and by age fifteen he was a mackerel fisherman. In his late teens he survived a shipwreck while aboard the *Enos B. Phillips,* which was ripped apart during a blizzard. Realizing the changing times from sail to steam he became a steamboat captain. A skilled boatman, he joined the Monomoy Life Saving Station in 1895, and was eventually promoted to Surfman Number 1 under the command of keeper Captain Eldredge.

Meanwhile, across the waters, Elmer F. Mayo on the barge *Fitzpatrick* noticed the capsized surfboat bobbing in the rough seas. He next noticed a lone surfman clinging to the boat and knew from his stints as a Cape life saver that a surfboat typically carried a crew of seven, so the magnitude of the disaster was quite evident. Mayo reacted quickly, and with only a fourteen-foot dory between himself and a watery grave rowed out toward the capsized surfboat.

Elmer Mayo, born in 1862 at Chatham, was a well-known Cape wrecker and anchor dragger, and was an expert boatman. His father was a life saving station keeper at Chatham and Mayo was a substitute life saver so he knew his way around a surfboat and breeches buoy. As a skilled wrecker in his schooner *Gleaner* he combed the shoals for sunken wrecks to see what treasures they held. Wrecks could offer a trove of valuable items: fishing nets, canvas sails, anchors, chains, navigational equipment, cleats, blocks, rope, and of course, the ship's cargo.

In March 1902, Mayo was hired to refloat the *Fitzpatrick*. Though most of the wrecking crew went ashore on the previous evening because of the rough seas, he and a small crew remained on board. The next morning, the fog was so thick he couldn't even see the barge *Wadena* stranded on the same shoal, nor did he know she was flying a distress signal. He was equally unaware of the rescue attempt from Monomoy Station.

Plucking the exhausted Ellis from certain death, Mayo headed the dory toward shore where stood Surfman Walter C. Bloomer, who did not accompany his comrades on the surfboat only because it was his day for kitchen duty. Not until he helped Mayo land the boat did he learn of the tragedy that now made him Surfman Number 1, while Ellis became the new keeper of the Monomoy station.

For "acts of extreme heroism" Mayo received citations from the Massachusetts Humane Society and the United States Government. He later left Cape Cod, first heading to the Klondike in search of gold, and then to Seattle for deep sea fishing. Later in life he returned to Chatham, dying in 1935, the same year as fellow Monomoy hero, Seth Ellis. With their passing, the drama which took place upon Shovelful Shoals three decades earlier had finally reached its conclusion.

Chapter 6

Independence

Cape Codders have always exhibited a bit of an independent streak, so it should really come as no surprise that when the flame of freedom was first lit many locals rose up to fan those flames into a revolution. In fact, the members of one West Barnstable family were key players during the Revolutionary period; James Otis, Jr. providing the spark of independence through his speeches and pamphlets, brother Joseph serving as a Revolutionary War general, and sister Mercy using her pen to help champion the Patriots' cause through her poems and plays. Surprisingly, when the matter came to a vote in 1776, Barnstable was one of only two towns in all of New England to vote against independence.

A Flame of Fire

In the annals of American history, the Otis family of Barnstable holds a special place in the great book of our country's birth and progress. Their influence was felt locally on Cape Cod and in Massachusetts as well as throughout the colonies. Colonel James Otis was a General Court representative and Governor's Councilor during the years leading up to the American Revolutionary War period. He and his wife, Mary Allyne Otis, had thirteen children, many that did not live past childhood, yet a number that went on to play important roles during the decades before, during, and after the Revolution.

Daughter Mercy Otis Warren became a political satirist, using her pen to poke fun at the crown through poetry and plays. The Colonel's

Barnstable Village statue of the Patriot James Otis, Jr. speaking out against the
Writs of Assistance in 1761. Photo: Jack Sheedy

son, Joseph, became a Revolutionary War general known for his quick
temper and wild behavior, while another son, Samuel, became the
country's first Secretary of the US Senate in 1789, holding the Bible
when George Washington took his oath of office, and holding the
position until his death in 1814. Yet it was son, James, Jr., who was
the impetus leading to all that was to follow as he was America's first
Patriot – before Samuel Adams, before John Hancock, before Patrick
Henry, before them all.

James Otis, Jr. was born on February 5, 1725 at West Barnstable; a
plaque on a boulder along Route 6A midway between routes 132 and 149
marks the location of the Otis homestead. A 1743 graduate of Harvard,
earning his master's degree in 1746, he went on to study law for the next
two years, practicing first at Barnstable, then at Plymouth, and finally
relocating to Boston. In 1755, after establishing a level of success with
his law practice, he married Ruth Cunningham, the daughter of a
Boston businessman. It would be Otis' eventual fight for the cause
of the colonial merchants that would elevate him to prominence and

make his name synonymous with the term "Patriot."

Otis earned the position of Advocate General of the Vice Admiralty Court, a position which had him upholding British rule, yet he soon felt his position was in direct conflict with his beliefs. He sided with the cause of the Boston merchants, but his role as Advocate General assisted the British in stifling the merchants' freedoms. In 1761 the spark of freedom flickered to life. It began with the death of King George II in 1760. As was typically done when a new king was crowned, the writs of the empire were renewed, which is what happened when George III took the throne. The Writs of Assistance were tightened like a noose around the colonists' necks, and it was Otis' job to defend these new laws. In response, Otis resigned his position as Advocate General to oppose the writs as counsel for the Boston merchants. The Advocate General became the Brits' adversary!

The new writs were written in an attempt to put further pressures on the colonies. The British suspected the colonists of violating the Navigational Acts, of smuggling illegal cargoes into the colonies, and of trading with the enemy during the French and Indian War. The writs made it legal for private homes, businesses, and ships at sea to be searched by customs officers at any time for any reason without a warrant. In opposition, in February 1761, Otis delivered his speech against the Writs of Assistance in the council chamber at Boston's Old State House. He spoke for four hours before a panel of judges including Lieutenant Governor Thomas Hutchinson, and with that famous speech lit the spark of revolution in the hearts of his compatriots. John Adams, who was present, later wrote: "Mr. Otis' oration breathed into this nation the breath of life ... then and there was the first scene of the first act of the opposition to the arbitrary claims of Great Britain ... American independence was then and there born."

Otis argued that the British writs were unlawful, yet his arguments transcended the issues of common law, maintaining that the writs were in violation of natural law and elevating the issue to political and philosophical levels, even speaking of human rights and denouncing slavery. Though no copies of the speech survived, those present described it as "eloquent," "impassioned," "momentous," and the product of "conclusive reasoning." Adams took notes and decades later, in his old age, attempted to reconstruct portions of Otis' oration. He later stated, "Otis was a flame of fire" and that he had "a prophetic glance of his eyes into futurity." Otis apparently made reference to "my country" when referring to the colonies, marking the first known instance of anyone conceiving of a nation separate and independent from the Crown. From that time forward, British rule was always questioned and scrutinized.

Otis became a nationally recognized Patriot, statesman, pamphleteer, and orator. He was elected to the General Court in 1761 as a representative from Boston and five years later was elected speaker although the royal governor disallowed his appointment due to his strong anti-British stance and his position against the Stamp Act. In 1764, he voiced his opposition to the Sugar Act by stating that "no parts of his Majesty's domain can be taxed without their consent." The following year he was one of the major colonial figures at the Stamp Act Congress, while he decried the Townshend Act by writing that "no one should be taxed without representation." He wrote a number of pamphlets and letters from 1764 to 1768 protesting British rule, some co-authored by other Boston Patriots, including Samuel Adams. These stances spawned enemies and a handful made their presence known in September 1769 when Otis was severely beaten by a group of British customs officials at the British Coffee House on State Street in Boston. Though he survived the attack, his skull was fractured. For the remainder of his life he would battle for his sanity, although there is some thought that perhaps he suffered mentally even before the attack. In either case, his sense of reasoning was impacted, though he enjoyed periods of lucid behavior reminiscent of his younger days of fire and flame. Yet, his lucidity could regress back to lunacy. In 1770 he went mad at the State House, breaking windows, burning his papers, and firing off a musket. He was judged a lunatic and his brother, Samuel, was named his guardian. Despite his condition, he served briefly in the legislature during 1771.

Later, Otis was removed to Lawrence Pond in Sandwich to stay at the home of family friend Joseph Lawrence, who agreed to watch over the former Patriot and orator. On a number of occasions Otis absented himself, turning up somewhere along the old carriage route between Barnstable and Boston, probably thinking he had speeches to deliver at the State House or pamphlets to write at his downtown office. According to local lore, upon one such disappearance, on June 17, 1775 he left his sister, Mercy's, home in Watertown and wound up at the Battle of Bunker Hill. In the early 1780s he was relocated to the farm of Isaac Osgood in Andover, Massachusetts where he spent the final two years of his life in a private apartment on the grounds.

On May 23, 1783, he was at Osgood's farm speaking to a small group of people who gathered to hear the "master," as John Adams later called him, recount stories of the pre-war years. As he spoke a storm blew in across the fields and out of the sky came a bolt of lightning, striking the Patriot and killing him. The great orator was finally silenced.

Since Otis' papers and the contents of his speeches were destroyed, sadly lost forever, his memory tends to elude the fame bestowed upon Patriots John and Samuel Adams, John Hancock, Paul Revere, and Patrick Henry. His mental condition prevented him from participating in the events leading up to the Declaration of Independence and the Revolutionary War to follow. Yet, Otis was one of the key characters in our country's battle for independence. He was there at the very beginning. In fact, one could argue that Otis *was* the very beginning, a decade and a half before the Declaration.

Shortly after Otis' death, the Treaty of Paris was signed between the newly formed United States and Great Britain. The revolution begun by James Otis' speech against the Writs of Assistance twenty-two years earlier had finally been won.

Mercy Otis Warren: Liberty's Penwoman

While James Otis, Jr. gets deserved credit for his patriotic activities, only more recently has Otis' sister, Mercy Otis Warren, been given recognition as playing a significant role in the struggle for liberty as both a writer of political satire and a confidant of a number of important Revolutionary personalities. Her plays, comedies, and essays, often written anonymously, can be viewed as a feminine version of what the more famous Thomas Paine was doing with his essays on liberty.

Mercy Otis was born in Barnstable on September 25, 1728. Her father, Pilgrim descendant James Otis, Sr., was a well-to-do merchant of some political and economic note in the colony. The elder Otis served as a member of the colonial Governor's Council. As such, the Otis

Statue of Mercy Otis Warren in Barnstable, depicting the great "penwoman" of the American Revolution. Photo: Jack Sheedy

household was often the scene of political discussion and interest in affairs beyond the local community.

One of thirteen children, Mercy was perhaps closest in temperament to her older brother, James. Although never formally schooled, she nevertheless developed an interest in reading and her tastes tended toward the classics and world issues. When her brother went off to Harvard, she continued a lively correspondence with him and in 1754 she married one of his classmates, the Plymouth aristocrat and Mayflower descendant, James Warren. This marriage lasted fifty-four years and produced five sons. Although her husband served in a number of official posts during the Revolutionary War, it was Mercy who became the more well-known and self-anointed feminine conscience of the independence movement.

As a satirist, her work lampooned the area Loyalists with stinging force. Her plays and melodramas cast thinly disguised leading members of the Boston Loyalist community as ruffians and buffoons and were outrageous in their pointed criticism of the British colonial

administration. Her works were designed as revolutionary propa-
ganda and were widely read and appreciated by men and women
who favored independence.

Not so much a pure feminist as she was a champion of colonial
liberty, Mercy cut across gender lines in calling for an end to British
political authority while urging women to actively boycott British
goods. Even though she clearly believed that a woman's intellect
could be equal to that of a man, she wrote consistently that she
considered a woman's role of domestic helpmate as being a higher
calling. But as her husband acknowledged, "She has a woman's
temperament, but a man's mind."

After the Revolution, all of Mercy's plays were published with her
name boldly printed on them and she enjoyed wide readership. It was
in these post-war years that Mercy Otis Warren began to establish
herself politically as a strong republican in the Jeffersonian sense.
She opposed the centralized power structure that came with the
1789 Constitution because she feared that it could allow a despotic
leader to seize control of the new nation. She championed the Bill of
Rights. This put her at odds with many of her former Massachusetts
Patriot contemporaries who were staunch Federalists, including John
Hancock, Samuel Adams, and John Adams.

In contrast to his early praise of her wartime literary effort, John
Adams referred to one of her later works as being "like mustard after
dinner." Much of his criticism was directed at her 1805 three-volume
publication of the first history of the Revolution entitled: *The History
of the Rise, Progress, and Termination of the American Revolution*. The
book, which covered the time from the Stamp Act controversy to
the beginning of the nineteenth century, contained a good deal of
anti-Federalist criticism, much of it directed at the second president's
recently concluded administration and Adams never fully forgave
her for it.

Eventually, in her final years, there was a rapprochement with many
of her political adversaries, including Adams. Mercy continued to
correspond about the issues of the day with people she had known
for more than half a century. She finished her days in Plymouth,
outliving her husband by six years, passing away at the age of eighty-
four in October of 1814. As a crusader for liberty, Mercy Otis Warren

demonstrated in her own special way that in a political struggle, the pen can certainly be as mighty as the sword.

Quarrel & Conflict

In the period leading up to the Declaration of Independence, the village of Barnstable was a village in conflict. Positions on the matter of independence were split, with Whigs tending their fields and digging their shellfish side-by-side with Tories. It is understandable that these Whigs and Tories of the same village did not share the same opinions of the day's events, but there is evidence to suggest that even the Whigs in Barnstable did not see eye-to-eye with one another as well.

Barnstable at that time was a cauldron of conflicting thought. The 1774 march against the courthouse seemed to suggest that the cause for independence was firmly rooted in the shire town, yet there was division amongst the villagers and within the town itself. In fact, the account of historian Amos Otis, who wrote *Genealogical Notes of Barnstable Families*, indicated that there were four divisions in the Cape town – passionate Whigs, moderate Whigs, passionate Tories, and moderate Tories. No matter which camp you were in, it seems, you had enemies in the other three.

Town records for May 1776 reference an address to be made by Colonel James Otis, the father of the Patriot. Apparently the esteemed Colonel was invited to speak before the assembly, but it was voted that they would not hear an apology on the "Crocker Quarrel," nor on the "Abigail Freeman Affair." The "Quarrel" and the "Affair" refer to two events that had recently taken place on the streets of the village.

The "Crocker Quarrel" in question occurred during a training exercise as Colonel Joseph Otis, brother of the Patriot, and Colonel Nathaniel Freeman ran the men through drills. The soldiers snubbed their commanding officers by refusing to follow their orders. Colonel Otis, an ardent Whig, immediately blamed the Crocker boys for the insubordinate action, barking at moderate Whig Captain Sam Crocker, "The Crockers are at the bottom of this!" After a further exchange of words Otis swung his cane at Crocker and a fight commenced.

Meanwhile, Colonel Freeman took on Cornelius Crocker, who owned the nearby Crocker Tavern. The argument between the two men went from the street and into the tavern, where an old-fashioned sword fight took place. Apparently Crocker was struck a number of times until his brother, Elijah, arrived with a musket. Fortunately, the fight was ended before anyone was killed.

There was certainly no shortage of opinions in the village of Barnstable where Whigs and Tories plowed their fields and drank their pints within shouting distance of one another. And it was in the midst of this environment, at about the same period as the Crocker Quarrel, that tempers boiled out of control once again, resulting in the tarring and feathering of Abigail Freeman.

Donald Trayser, in his book *Barnstable: Three Centuries of a Cape Cod Town*, described Freeman as "an outspoken shrewish Tory." Known around the village of Barnstable as Widow Nabby, she ran a general store in which she let her opinions fly from behind the counter. She also had no problem voicing her Loyalist sentiments out on the streets of the village, regardless of whether the person standing before her was Whig or Tory.

At her store she continued to sell British tea, which, because of its high tax, was boycotted by the Patriots. Yet, she was not alone in town in terms of her Loyalist views; others holding her opinion against breaking with the crown included Donald Parker, Jesse Cobb, tavern owner Otis Loring, and Edward Bacon. Yet, Widow Nabby's fierce Tory stance, and perhaps her big mouth, put her at odds with a number of her fellow villagers, quickly making her the target of their aggression.

According to local lore, a gang of young men entered Freeman's house one night, took her from her bed, and hauled her out into the street. There, she was tarred and feathered and then carried around the streets on a rail. The process of "tarring and feathering" consisted of stripping a person, smearing their skin with a sticky pine tar substance, and then rolling them in feathers. It could take days to remove all the feathers and tar. The process was meant to publicly humiliate the victim, with this episode representing the only recorded case in Barnstable, and probably on all of Cape Cod. It was certainly a low point in Barnstable's struggle for independence.

Tempers eventually cooled over the months that followed, although the occasional toppling of a Liberty Pole reminded residents that differing views prevailed in the village of Barnstable.

On Independency, Barnstable Voted "No!!"

In the decisive days before the adoption of the Declaration of Independence, a number of Cape Cod towns held town meetings to discuss the adoption or rejection of the document.

Harwich held its meeting on June 17, 1776 and voted that its representatives to the General Court should support independence. Wellfleet endorsed the document the same week. Despite its exposed position on the Outer Cape, Truro voted for independence on June 18, 1776. Two days later in Yarmouth, the citizens voted unanimously "that the inhabitants of the town of Yarmouth do declare a state of independence of the King of Great Britain, agreeably to a late resolve of the General Court, if in case the wisdom of Congress should see proper to do it."

In Barnstable, however, there was considerable support for the position of the Crown. As the shire town and the birthplace of the Patriot James Otis, Jr., one would think that the Cape's largest and most influential town would have been a leader in the adoption of the Declaration of Independence. Indeed the 1774 march to Barnstable of the "Body of the People," a group of Patriots who strongly objected to the King's tampering with the jury system, indicated that there was a substantial group of citizens who took issue with England's colonial rule.

But some wealthy and influential Barnstable Tories, led by Edward Bacon, so intimidated the voters at the June 25 meeting that a large number refused even to vote on the question of supporting the Declaration. The "rump" remainder tallied thirty citizens in favor of independence and thirty-five opposed. Independence was defeated. Barnstable was only the second town in all of New England, the other being Ridgefield, Connecticut, that failed to produce a positive vote for independence.

The next day, a vigorous protest letter was sent to Boston, signed by twenty-three Barnstable Patriots who demanded another vote and who pledged their support for independence. They wrote "to let posterity know that there were a few in this town who dared stand forth in favor of an injured and oppressed country . . . and it is a matter of great grief to us that the Cause of Liberty is treated with such indignity by some of the inhabitants of the town of Barnstable." The after-the-fact letter mattered little to the General Court who stripped Barnstable of its representation in that legislative body until the war was almost over.

Perhaps what is even more curious is that despite the discontent that followed the vote against the Declaration of Independence, Edward Bacon, the chief Loyalist opponent of the document, was re-elected to the General Court as Barnstable's representative. He was denied a seat by the General Court in 1778 and yet he was re-elected again in 1780 and finally, despite his unfailing Tory sentiments, he was allowed to take his seat in the legislature. The voters of Barnstable apparently saw no inconsistency in continuing to support and elect a representative during the war who continued to declare his opposition to the break with England.

Two Unsung Revolutionary Heroes

The drive for American independence produced a number of active participants from Cape Cod. First and foremost was James Otis, Jr. whose fiery speeches against British rule put him in the forefront of the Patriot cause. But there were other local luminaries like Falmouth's Joseph Dimmick, a captain in the town militia who, through clever subterfuge, captured several British ships anchored in the Elizabeth Islands. And there was Colonel Nathaniel Freeman of Sandwich who led a group of Patriots in a successful effort to close the King's court in Barnstable. Throughout the conflict there were hundreds of local men, less known, who left their homes to fight for liberty.

Two Patriots with connections to the Cape rarely get a mention in most history books. One was a behind-the-scenes spy who was never recognized for his wartime contributions and the other was so much an overt and feisty Patriot that Theodore Roosevelt in his 1906 history of the Revolution referred to him as "a frothy man, a noisy braggart, a demagogue and mob leader."

Born in Harwich in 1749, Enoch Crosby was an unlikely hero. At age 21 he moved to Danbury, Connecticut where he became an itinerant shoemaker. When war broke out, Crosby attempted to enlist in the Continental Army. Patriot officials convinced him that he could be more valuable moving around repairing Loyalist shoes and secretly gathering information about the enemy. He travelled frequently between New York, Connecticut, and Massachusetts making lists of Loyalists and noting the positions and strengths of British troops. Crosby passed this information to the Patriot side. At one point he was compromised and his mission became so dangerous that he was removed from spying. Still wanting to make a contribution, Crosby enlisted in the army and served until the war's conclusion. His important role unknown for years, Crosby was finally recognized near the end of his life when author, James Fenimore Cooper, wrote a best-selling novel – *The Spy*. Cooper's main character was based on Crosby's wartime clandestine activities. Only then did the public acknowledge and give long overdue credit to this son of Cape Cod.

A larger than life personality with Cape roots was West Brewster-born Isaac Sears who later achieved notoriety in New York City as the founder of the Sons of Liberty there. In 1765, he came to the attention of the local Patriots after a series of speeches against the Stamp Act. Recognized as much for his fists as for his speechmaking abilities, Sears rose steadily in the Patriot hierarchy in New York to the point where, because of his strong leadership in the independence movement, people referred to him as "King Sears." In 1774 he led a tea party protest similar to the one in Boston and there is evidence that he was one of the men who pulled down the statue of King George on July 1, 1776. Forced to leave New York when the British occupied the city, Sears moved back to Massachusetts and was an important financial backer of privateers sailing from Boston. The war bankrupted him and he died on a voyage to China in 1786 while trying to regain his fortune.

Chapter 7

At War

Cape Codders have played a role in every American military conflict – even back in the years before the formation of the United States – in fact, all the way back to the King Philip's War of 1675-76. And the peninsula of Cape Cod was the venue for a number of military encounters during the Revolutionary War and the War of 1812, as well as a minor skirmish during World War I when a German U-boat surfaced off Orleans. And, of course, local men answered the call during the Civil War, participating in every major engagement. Through it all, Cape Codders rose to the challenge in defense of their country.

Falmouth Under Attack

Cape Cod's unique position some forty miles out to sea rendered her exposed to British attack during the Revolutionary War. With her ports blockaded, her ships were seized and her crops and livestock were stolen. Cape Codders had a choice – either give in to British demands or else put up a defense. One town that chose to fight was Falmouth. The town seemed constantly at odds with the British and regularly fired upon her ships passing along the coast. It helped that Falmouth had a strong military leader in Captain Joseph Dimmick, who challenged the greatest navy in the world, and was victorious.

The British fleet landed at Falmouth on April 2, 1779, coming ashore with the intent of stealing provisions. The local militia arrived and drove the marauders back to their base at Tarpaulin Cove on Naushon Island. That night, at a tavern owned by Tory John Slocum, the British made plans to take their revenge on Falmouth the next day by burning the town. Slocum, who had a change of allegiance, sent his son across Vineyard Sound in a dory to warn Captain Dimmick of the Falmouth militia, who then mustered his men and had entrenchments dug along the beach, readied for attack.

The next morning, two British schooners and eight sloops appeared off the coast prepared to bombard Falmouth. From morning until late afternoon cannonballs flew overhead. More than two hundred British soldiers attempted to make landfall, yet the Falmouth men held them off. Captain Dimmick called for reinforcements from neighboring towns and men from Sandwich later joined his forces; the Barnstable militia was on its way but received word they were no longer needed. The British withdrew and later attempted a landing further west at Woods Hole but without success as Dimmick sent forces to protect the beach.

Afterwards, he decided to go on the offensive. He drew up plans to win back a Falmouth schooner full of corn stolen by the British. At that time a schooner full of food was especially valuable as Cape ports were blocked and Cape towns were being pillaged to feed the British forces. The captain of the schooner had escaped and apprised Dimmick of the situation. So, before daybreak he took three whaleboats full of Falmouth militia into Tarpaulin Cove where they came upon the British fleet. At sunrise, as they approached the hijacked schooner, the British fired upon the whaleboats. The Falmouth men responded with gunfire and were successful in boarding the schooner, yet in the confusion of battle ran her aground. Fighting off the British all the while, they waited for high tide to lift the vessel free, which they eventually sailed back to Woods Hole.

Later, Dimmick took a crew of twenty-five men to Vineyard Haven Harbor. Under the veil of darkness, he and his men engaged the British schooner *General Leslie*. Although the British out-gunned and out-manned him, he was successful in capturing the vessel, sailing her back to Hyannis along with a number of British prisoners he captured in the process.

The War of 1812

The War of 1812 doesn't get all that much mention in the history

A cannon dating to the War of 1812 located outside the Barnstable County Courthouse. It was brought to Barnstable to protect the village against a possible British attack. Photo: Jack Sheedy.

books. If mentioned at all, the record celebrates Francis Scott Key's vision of Fort McHenry with the bombs bursting and the flag that was still there. Also mentioned are the sea victories of the *U.S.S. Constitution* -- "Old Ironsides" and Dolley Madison's dramatic rescue of the portrait of George Washington from the burning White House. But for Cape Codders, the so-called "second war of independence" had real consequences. Plagued by a tight naval blockade that ruined the economy and caused near starvation, the description of the conflict can probably be best summed up in a Yarmouth town meeting resolution in the spring of 1814 that called the struggle with Britain quite accurately, a "ruinous and unhappy war." As Cape historian Henry Kittredge has written, "No part of the state was more hard hit than Cape Cod. Her fishermen could no longer carry their fares to foreign ports and half their vessels lay rotting once more at abandoned wharfs. The villages were filled with idle men who spent their days in vehement and not always very intelligent invective against the Administration."

Initially some Cape towns actually favored war with Britain. Sandwich, Barnstable, Falmouth, and Orleans had majorities in favor. And there was enough patriotism on the Cape to muster a resolution at a county congress praising the Madison administration. "We have the fullest confidence in the wisdom, firmness, and patriotism of the president and congress of whom doings we cordially approve."

But even as war clouds gathered, there was apprehension about what might happen should America go to war against the world's greatest maritime power. Chatham passed a resolution expressing "an unwillingness and disapprobation to enter into the present war." Part of the town's concern was "an abhorrence of the people to any alliance with France." And in the fall elections of 1812, Cape towns emphatically expressed their disapproval at the ballot box. With large majorities, they returned Governor Caleb Strong, a Federalist and anti-war leader, to office. Typical was Chatham's vote for Strong -- 95 to only 29 for the war candidate Joseph Varnum.

From the outset, the enemy was clearly visible to Cape Codders. *HMS Nymph* and *HMS Bulwark* controlled the upper Cape and Plymouth regions of Cape Cod Bay. *HMS Nimrod* patrolled the area of Nantucket Sound and the Islands. The British frigates *Majestic* and *Spencer* occupied Provincetown Harbor, effectively cutting off all communication between the Cape and Boston. Cape Codders ran the gauntlet at their peril. "Jeremiah's Gutter," a small canal connecting the Bay with Nauset Harbor, was put back in service for local trade—mostly whaleboats of shallow draft. The old portage route from Scusset River across to the Manomet River in Buzzards Bay was also reactivated. (It would be a century before the Cape Cod Canal was built.) But accommodation with the situation seemed to be the best option. Some felt that the willingness to do business with the enemy bordered on treason. Occupying British forces at the Cape tip found a steady supply of locally produced food at their disposal. And they paid in specie—hard currency, not with paper money. Shebnah Rich, a Truro historian, noted that, "Provincetown received no small benefit from the English vessels, and some of the fortunes since acquired, had their beginnings from this source." Rich added that "The officers often landed, visited the houses, were always very civil, and became well acquainted with a good many families.

They purchased butter, milk, eggs, chickens and other supplies and secured small repairs as needed, paying for them quite liberally with British gold." The captain of *HMS Majestic* had a similar assessment. "The inhabitants of Provincetown are disposed to be on friendly terms, and have promised water and on reasonable terms, fish, fruit and vegetables." Another British officer noted wryly that "the local selectmen are indeed select as they visit our ships with select cuts of local beef." Wellfleet officials teamed up with their counterparts in Chatham to supply sheep. There were charges that local people put profits over patriotism in their dealing with the British. And there may have been some truth in this. "Begin with a dollar and proceed to any amount. You can always buy a Yankee," one British officer observed.

Some Cape men took to privateering as a way of getting at the British. Operating from small sloops and schooners, attacks at sea against British commerce could be profitable but had considerable risks. Mulford Harding of Chatham was a member of the privateer *Reindeer,* which was captured by the British. He spent months in Dartmoor Prison before the war ended and he was able to return home. He shared space in the prison on the south coast of England with a number of other Cape Codders including Captain Zenas Bassett of Hyannis, and George Lovell and Charles Boult of Osterville. Others who served time at Dartmoor were a group of Truro sailors including David Snow, Samuel Smith, William White, and Joseph Dyer.

With the defeat of Napoleon in 1814, the British were able to turn their attention from Europe to America. This was the year that saw a major escalation of incidents and incursions around Cape Cod. The British were using Tarpaulin Cove on Naushon Island as a headquarters and their vessels frequently passed close to the Falmouth shoreline. The Falmouth militia had several cannons mounted on the beach and the British sent a demand that they be given up. Rather than do this, the town challenged the British to come and get them. In January of 1814, *HMS Nimrod,* an 18-gun "cruiser," moved in close and after a gentlemanly warning of two hours to allow people to flee, fired about 300 cannon shots into the village. Some thirty dwellings suffered light damage. The Falmouth militia, aided by men from Sandwich and Barnstable, stood fast and ready. But the British prudently decided against putting soldiers ashore. The cannonade, which lasted into the early evening, proved ineffective and the British departed. Falmouth resident Ichabod Hatch reportedly ducked when a cannonball went through the front door of his house. He was said to have shouted "There, Damn Ye, John Bull. See if you can do it again." Hatch narrowly missed death as a second ball hit near where he was standing. The *Nimrod* would do much more damage five months later in nearby Wareham when, in June, in conjunction with the 74-gun *HMS Superb*, 220 British Marines attacked the village. Some of the town's leading figures were kidnapped to insure the safety of the invading forces. Five vessels were destroyed and the town's cotton mill was burned with damages estimated at $40,000.

Clearly aware of what happened in neighboring Wareham, Sandwich convened a special town meeting on June 22nd. Voters approved a measure whereby a Committee of Safety, consisting of 15 volunteers, was set up "to keep a watch on the seashore." Signals were placed on high hills such as Pine Hill in Pocasset and on the ridge over Bournedale to warn the local populace of a possible British land incursion. Less than three months later at a meeting on September 21st, Sandwich voters acted to "take any measures to defend themselves against the common enemy." The language of the article said that "the inhabitants will defend their houses and firesides and their families to the last extremity." A petition was sent to Governor Strong asking for 150 men to be sent to Sandwich and "fifty stand of arms, and two six pound field pieces with ammunition and equipment." Nathan Nye and Elisha Perry were charged with going to Boston to collect the arms.

Further down Cape the apprehension was the same. The Wellfleet militia was called out on July 8, 1814 when the captain of *HMS Nymph* threatened to "lay the town to ashes and burn every vessel belonging thereto," if he did not immediately see one of his men repatriated after the sailor had been captured aboard a sloop in the bay. An exchange was worked out. In September of 1814, Eastham and Brewster paid $1,200 and $4,000, respectively, to keep their salt works from being burned by the British warship *HMS Spencer*. Paying up was deemed preferable to doing battle with the superior British. Some towns did put up a show of resistance to British incursions. Barnstable raised four cannons at Salten Point to block a British attack on their salt works. It was as much bluff as anything else. The captain of *HMS Nymph* was probably more intimidated by the dangerous tidal range and shoals off Barnstable Harbor than he was by the show of strength by the local militia forces. When Sandwich was menaced by *HMS Commodore Hardy* in September, there was little that local forces could do when the warship fired some cannonballs at the brick kiln located on Town Neck, incorrectly thinking it was a fortress.

Historical placard honoring the "Battle of Rock Harbor" in 1814. Photo: Jack Sheedy

When in July of 1814 the *HMS Nymph* arrived off Bass River, the officer in charge of the warship warned the citizens of South Yarmouth that if the village didn't come up with $1,000 he would burn the town. The small Quaker community had little in the way of resources to pay the ransom. They devised a plan where they sent a simple man by the name of Abner Crowell out to the ship with a note pinned to his coat advising the British that all of the townspeople were like "Uncle Abner" and in a "distressed condition." Local lore says that the British accepted the ruse and agreed that they would spare the village. Furthermore, they agreed that any fishing vessel carrying a pass from "Uncle Abner" would be allowed to fish unmolested as long as there was no demonstration of acting against British interests.

At Orleans on December 19th 1814, *HMS Newcastle* went aground at low tide on the bay flats. The crew managed to get the vessel off by throwing off ship's stores, some of which floated into Rock Harbor. To retrieve their lost equipment, the British mounted an attack on the small harbor where they were met by the Orleans militia and while the attackers did manage to capture a schooner and three small sloops—burning two of them, they were eventually repulsed with a single casualty. This action became known ever after in Cape lore as the Battle of Rock Harbor. As a result of that action, some British sailors were taken prisoner a few days after the skirmish when one of the captured sloops grounded at low tide off the Yarmouth flats. It was the last active engagement of the war for Cape Cod. Ironically, the battle took place only five days before the peace treaty that ended hostilities was signed in Ghent. Because of the difficulty of communication, Americans didn't learn of the war's end immediately. When General Andrew Jackson defeated the British at New Orleans on January 8, 1815, the war had been over for two weeks.

1812 Tricksters

Cape Cod folklore is sprinkled with a degree of salt. For instance, there's no telling how much truth there is in these tales of the War of 1812 involving Cape Codders who put one over on their British adversaries, but these stories certainly point to Yankee ingenuity.

• • •

British Commodore Richard Ragget, aboard the warship *H.M.S. Spenser,* was harassing the Cape coast, blockading ports, and demanding ransoms from towns to save their salt works from bombardment. Attempting to run the blockade in a whaleboat full of provisions were two deep water ship masters, Captain Matthew Hopheny "Hoppy" Mayo and Captain Winslow L. Knowles. They were captured and Mayo was forced to act as pilot of a Yankee vessel seized by the British with orders to navigate the ship up the coast to Wellfleet. Mayo complied, but he had a plan, and aided by a patch of stormy weather, he set his plan in motion.

Claiming that the storm and the shoals made continuing any further dangerous, he convinced the British to anchor the vessel off Eastham and then managed to get the entire crew below decks with enough rum to get them all fairly drunk. Up top, by himself, Mayo rounded up all the weapons and tossed them overboard, except for two pistols which he put in his jacket. Next, he cut the anchor line and allowed the ship to drift with the storm until it ran aground at low tide. When the crew finally emerged on deck they discovered Mayo with the pistols drawn. He then climbed over the side of the vessel and walked across the flats to land where he mustered a group of Eastham men who followed him out to the grounded vessel and took the entire British crew captive. The prisoners were then marched to a local tavern where the Yanks and British raised pints together. Afterwards, the British were taken to a barn where they spent the remainder of the night. Yet, the next morning they escaped and stole back the Yankee vessel.

• • •

Born during the Revolutionary War, Joshua Crosby of Orleans went to sea at the age of thirteen aboard a fisherman, later sailing on whalers and coastal schooners, but he would be remembered for his service aboard the American warship *USS Constitution*. Trained on whalers as a gunner battling pirates off the Barbary Coast, this experience would serve him well when he became a quarterdeck gunnery officer on the *Constitution*, on which his most memorable battle took place on August 19, 1812 when *"Old Ironsides"* engaged the British warship *HMS Guerriere* off the coast of Massachusetts. This encounter resulted in a Yankee victory, the first major American victory of the war. Crosby's efforts helped deliver a key assault against the *Guerriere* that eventually resulted in the victory as Crosby trained his gun on the mizzenmast, bringing it down and causing the British to surrender less than thirty minutes later.

Interestingly, there is a side story to this battle that concerns a barrel of molasses on board the *Guerriere's* deck, which may have contributed to the victory. Molasses was used to concoct a "landlubber's" drink called switchel and for a seafarer to be offered this drink was considered an insult of the highest order. In anticipation of a victory, the *Guerriere's* crew rolled a barrel of molasses up top in view of the Americans – the 19th century's way of thumbing your nose at the opposition. Yet the move backfired on the British as the *Constitution's* gunners destroyed the barrel, thus spilling its slippery contents all over the *Guerriere's* deck, making it nearly impossible for the British to keep their footing and maneuver their vessel.

The Civil War monument in the village of Centerville, honoring those who fought and gave the supreme sacrifice in the War of the Rebellion. Photo: Jack Sheedy.

Cape Cod and the War of the Rebellion

When the Civil War came in the middle of the 19th century, Cape Codders were already struggling with the great questions of the day relating to national unity and slavery. Despite the rural and semi-isolated nature of the Cape, inhabitants were not unaware of the growing regional tensions that created two separate societies in the nation.

The coasting trade, dominated by New England vessels, connected the economies of the north and south and sailing crews brought back firsthand knowledge of how the country was evolving into two very different camps. Cape Codders in the nineteenth century were surprisingly literate and were kept abreast of national events by a wide arrangement of newspapers and pamphlets.

As to the institution of slavery, it existed on a small scale in New England up through the eighteenth century. The economy, which was fully centered on free labor and industry, ruled out the widespread use of slaves although there are plenty of local records that show Cape Codders owned personal "servants" as late as the first years of the nineteenth century. There was ambivalence on the part of most Cape Codders when it came to placing moral judgments on those who endorsed the "peculiar institution." Since it was the law of the land, the majority was generally content to leave slavery where it existed.

Some churches split over the contradiction of slavery and the message of Christianity, but save for the Quaker commu-

Major Charles Chipman of Sandwich
Photo courtesy of the Sandwich Historical
Society/Sandwich Glass Museum
Photographer: Robert Lee Ward

nity in Falmouth there was never a strong local abolitionist sentiment. Indeed, some of the worst riots over the slavery question happened on the Cape in the 1840s when abolitionists attempted to hold rallies in Harwich. They were beaten and run out of town by citizens who felt that it was an issue for southerners to decide. Certainly there were committed abolitionists, like Captain Jonathan Walker of Harwich, who risked their lives to bring escaped slaves north to freedom, and there was a small but well organized chapter of the Underground Railroad on the Cape. But these individuals and organizations were exceptions and the issue of slavery incited little fervor.

On the second and larger issue of Union, there was, however, no ambivalence. When the first rebel shots were fired on Fort Sumter in the spring of 1861, there was a swell of enthusiasm for God, Father Abraham, and Union. Each Cape Cod town was quickly able to fill the initial quota for troops. Captain Charles Chipman led a contingent of "three months men," called the "Sandwich Guards," to Boston where they were immediately moved south to be in place to defend Washington, D.C. Large amounts of money were pledged by each town in spring town meetings for the support of what was expected to be a short and glorious expedition.

Cape Cod might have been expected to make its major contribution in providing enlistments for the navy. In fact, volunteers seemed to be generally split between the army and the navy. In both services, hundreds of volunteers passed the four years of the conflict with a combination of long periods of boredom and loneliness coupled with short, intense moments of terror and blood. Beginning with Bull Run in the early days of the war, to the final surrender of Lee's army at Appomattox Courthouse in Virginia, Cape men were involved in all of the major campaigns.

Some men were wounded and ended their war service as invalids. Others suffered multiple wounds and continued to serve in the line for the duration of the war. John Ryder of Brewster saw action from 1862 until being wounded at Kenesaw Mountain in 1864. He survived the conflict and lived until 1929. Captain Chipman, who led the first contingent from the county, reached the rank of Lt. Colonel and died of wounds suffered in the siege of Petersburg in August of 1864.

Others, like Henry Knippe of Sandwich, Solomon Doane and Jonathan Gifford of Harwich, Benjamin Lombard of Truro, and Zabina Dill of Chatham, died in the infamous Andersonville, South Carolina Confederate prison. Cold Harbor, Fredericksburg, Chancellorsville, Petersburg, and Vicksburg were just some of the battlefields that claimed the lives of Cape Codders. In all, almost three thousand men served in the Union forces during the Civil War. This was almost ten percent of the population of the Cape at that time.

The exposed geography of Cape Cod posed a possible danger from Confederate privateers throughout the war years. Ship captains, such as Benjamin Howes of Dennis who saw his beautiful clipper *Southern Cross* captured and burned by the raider *Florida*, and Eastham's Captain Edward Penniman, who barely escaped having his New Bedford whaler *Minerva* sunk by the *Shenandoah*, were living testimony to the possibility of a rebel attack at sea. Captain Franklin Percival lost his ship *Charles Hill* to the Confederate privateer *Alabama* while sailing off the coast of South America.

Concerned about its vulnerability, Provincetown prevailed on the national government to build two forts on Long Point. These structures were later named "Fort Useless" and "Fort Harmless" as the threat of rebel invasion failed to materialize. Benjamin F. Robbins of Harwich noted in his journal that a Confederate raid on Cape Cod was unlikely, but he did cite an instance where a stranded steamer fired some cannons in Nantucket Sound, putting the town in a panic.

A few individuals rose to prominence during the war as a result of their exploits. Ezra C. Baker of Barnstable was given a field commission for bravery at Cold Harbor when he risked his life to bring his dead commander off the battlefield. Prentice H. Davis, also of Barnstable, served with the 24th Massachusetts Regiment and was decorated for gallant conduct at Morris Island. Sergeant Richard Lombard of Truro saw action in twenty-seven battles and skirmishes and was officially cited twice for bravery.

Joseph E. Hamblin, who was born in Yarmouth, was given a battlefield promotion to Brevet Brigadier General on the recommendation of General Phil Sheridan after valorous service in the major battles of Antietam, Fredericksburg, and Chancellorsville. Hamblin became the highest-ranking Cape Codder in the Union army. He was on active duty for the duration of the war, save for a few months while recovering from wounds suffered at Cedar Creek. But the vast majority of soldiers and sailors served their enlistments in obscurity, grateful that they were able to survive the appalling slaughter that marked the conflict.

The Civil War had effects on the economy and society of Cape Cod that lasted far beyond the conflict. Fisheries were very much reduced during the war, as were the traditional markets that supported maritime enterprise along the Atlantic coast. The merchant marine never returned to its prominence. A strong pre-war whaling industry also went into a decline. Subsequent post-war economic woes, which continued into the twentieth century, saw a slow but steady reduction in the population of the peninsula as young people moved away for better opportunities.

The experience of the war was never forgotten. Books were written and memorials constructed to commemorate the great national fratricide that came to be known in the North as the War of the Rebellion. Long after the struggle ended, veterans of the Grand Army of the Republic mustered annually in parades and reunions. It was at these gatherings that old warriors exchanged stories about lost youth and the war that changed the destiny of the nation.

U-boat Attack

After midnight on July 21, 1918, the nearly one hundred and forty-foot long tugboat *Perth Amboy* chugged into Gloucester Harbor with two coal barges in tow. At Gloucester she picked up another barge and then left the harbor on a southerly track to pick up a fourth barge – all four barges being more than one hundred and fifty feet long, with the largest being about one hundred and ninety feet. Their route would be taking them along the outer coastline of the Cape and a rendezvous with history.

Master of the *Perth Amboy* was Captain Joe Tapley. His wife was along for the trip as well. In their wake, on board the barge *Lansford* were Captain Charles Ainsleigh, his wife, and their ten-year-old son, Jack. Meanwhile, across the water on barge *No. 740* were Captain Joe Perry, his wife, and their daughter. Perry's crewman also brought along his family. The other two barges were *No. 703* and *No. 766*; in total, there were more than thirty people aboard the five vessels with about a quarter of them being women and children.

Daybreak found them off the Highland cliffs, near Cape Cod Light, and by 10:30 a.m. they were about three miles off Orleans and about ten miles from the Orleans Coast Guard Station. Typical for a July morning, there was a slight fog upon the water. On board the families were enjoying a leisurely cruise upon a peaceful Sunday morning. The women on board barge *No. 740* were preparing breakfast when the calm morning erupted with a sudden explosion.

On the eastern horizon a German U-boat, more than two hundred feet in length and armed with two deck guns, had surfaced and was firing upon the defenseless armada. The wooden barges didn't stand much of a chance against the barrage of nearly one hundred and fifty shells fired upon them. The crews hastily abandoned ship and watched as three of the barges, *No. 703, No. 740* and *No. 766*, disappeared beneath the waves. The final barge, *Lansford,* lasted longer, sinking on the following day. Captain Ainsleigh suffered injuries to both his arms when a shell exploded on board his barge while his son, Jack, it has been told, grabbed a .22 caliber rifle and fired at the German submarine. It is also said that the boy saved the American flag from the *Lansford* when they abandoned ship. The *Perth Amboy*, with its steel hull, survived the attack though her deck was riddled with holes and she was left burning, her crew leaving in lifeboats.

Although the newly completed Chatham naval air base was only ten miles away, many of the men were at a baseball game in Provincetown that morning. Eventually, one plane went up to repel the invaders by tossing tools, notably a monkey wrench, at the escaping U-boat. Soon the German vessel submerged and the US plane returned to base.

During the course of the attack, Captain Robert Pierce of the Chatham Coast Guard Station telephoned up to Provincetown to speak with his supervisor as he was unsure about what to do in a situation such as this. He knew he should launch a surfboat to save the survivors of the sinking vessels, but he was not sure if he could order his men to enter a battle in progress. The word came down from Provincetown to launch his boat and land the survivors. When Pierce and his crew arrived at the scene one of the barges had already been sunk and the crews of the barges and the tugboat were in lifeboats. The U-boat was still firing upon the *Perth Amboy* and the three remaining barges as well as at the beach. Pierce assessed the situation and decided that the injured – *Lansford* Captain Ainsleigh and a *Perth Amboy* crewman with a serious wound on his arm – needed to be brought ashore right away. So, he took the injured personnel on board his surfboat and headed toward the beach, urging the others in the lifeboats to follow after him. Everyone was safely landed.

Hundreds of people on shore lined the beaches to watch the events. Churches opened their doors early when news of the attack was learned. With so many witnesses accounts differed greatly. Some reports stated the ordeal lasted a half-hour while others reported an hour and a half as the duration. Some accounts said that one shell hit the beach, making Orleans the only place in the United States to be attacked during World War I, while others stated that a number of shells hit the beach and some hit the marsh beyond. The German

U-boat, it was said, fired about one hundred and fifty shells although some reports give a figure of less than one hundred. All, though, agreed that the Germans were rather poor shots.

The wounded were treated and eventually transported to Boston, and the *Perth Amboy* was towed to New York for repairs. And the waves erased all evidence of the vessels involved in the events of July 21, 1918, and the first attack against American soil since the War of 1812.

Chapter 8

Lost and Found

Not all that Cape Cod offers can be easily found along her worn and beaten paths. And not all of her history is easily accessible, thus requiring some digging about like an archeologist scraping away layers of dirt to uncover that which rests beneath. The Cape's legendary tales would fill countless volumes and would provide many years of reading for those interested in such research and discovery. Here are but a few stories, pointing to Cape Cod history that hints of tales both lost and found along the less travelled paths and back roads of a storied past.

Died with the Smallpox

Smallpox has been the scourge of humanity since prehistoric times. On Cape Cod, throughout the centuries, there were serious outbreaks and the early settlers and even the Natives were not immune to its ravages. In fact, smallpox was one of the contributing factors leading to the annihilation of the Cape and Islands Natives, leaving tribes only in Mashpee and at Aquinnah on Martha's Vineyard.

A viral disease resembling cowpox, smallpox was highly infectious and could be contracted by either direct contact with a carrier or by touching the bedclothes or clothing of someone infected. Between 30 and 40 percent of those who contracted smallpox died. In the days before medicines there was no treatment for the disease, only bed rest, fluids, and sedatives to make the victim as comfortable as possible. If the victim survived, their skin would most likely be permanently marked by the pox. The only preventive method was the isolation of the sick from the other members of the village, the quick burial of the deceased, and the burning or burial of the victim's clothing and bedclothes. So feared was the pox that those who died from the disease were buried by family members on their property rather than in the village cemetery. Or, in the case of large epidemics, the dead were buried in a designated plot for smallpox victims.

A tour of these smallpox cemeteries can be a somber journey – lonely headstones in nearly forgotten spots, separated from the rest of the population. The first visit is to the grave of a Chatham doctor who fought the dreaded disease that ravaged his fellow townsfolk, and in the end he, too, succumbed. Along the side of Training Field Road rests his stone, no more than a couple of feet from the street and the roar of automobiles, their occupants perhaps unaware of its historical significance. The stone reads: *"Here lies buried Dr. Samuel Lord who died of smallpox after devoted service to the citizens of Chatham in the epidemic of 1765-66."*

Not far from Dr. Lord's grave rest a number of his patients in a designated smallpox cemetery off Old Comers Road. In a wooded lot, perhaps one hundred feet in from the road, are a half dozen stones encircled with concrete posts supporting metal rails. The dates on the headstones point to the months from December 1765 to March 1766 when ten percent of the town's population contracted the disease; twenty-four of those infected survived while thirty-seven died. Considered one of the Cape's worst outbreaks, it is believed the pestilence arrived in Chatham in either a shipment of clothing from the West Indies or a bale of cotton from a southern colony. Normally, smallpox was detected early and was then contained to a handful of infected persons or a family or two, but in the Chatham case it somehow spread unabated until it reached epidemic proportions. The disease claimed not only the local doctor but also a doctor from neighboring Harwich. During one week, between January 11 and 17, seventeen people died, prompting the arrival of Boston physicians to town. The horror finally ended with the death of Mrs. Mehitabel Rider on March 20th.

At the cemetery on Old Comers Road there is a stone belonging to *"Mrs. Mercy Doane, the wife of Mr. Joseph Doane Junior, She Dec'd*

This smallpox cemetery in Yarmouth Port, dating to the early 19th century, is appropriately located on the 13th hole at the Kings Way Golf Course and contains the ashes of two victims of the disease. Photo: Jack Sheedy.

with the smallpox Jan'ry ye 6th 1766 in ye 25th year of her age." Another stone belongs to Deacon Stephen Smith, who died on January 13 at the age of sixty. Next to him is his wife who fell victim to the disease just three days later: *"Here lies buried Mrs. Bathsheba Smith, widow to Mr. Stephen Smith, who Dec'd in ye 57th year of her age with the smallpox, She Dec'd Jan'ry ye 16th 1766."* They also lost two daughters to the disease. Nearby rests Stephen Rider who, along with his wife and nine of their ten children, *"died with the smallpox."*

Other smallpox graves dot the Cape. For instance, those golfing at the Kings Way course in Yarmouth Port can view two graves on the 13th hole, just a short pitching wedge shot from the green. Encircled with a rusted chain draping from granite posts driven into the four corners of the small plot are the headstones of a John Hall, who died on December 14, 1801 at the age of sixty-four, and a person by the name of Taylor (the stone is largely illegible). In fact, the pox was such a problem at the beginning of the nineteenth century, at the time of the outbreak that took Hall's life, that the town of Yarmouth voted to build a smallpox inoculation house on Great Island in Nantucket Sound, far from the population of the town.

At the Cape tip, Provincetown, with its seafaring traffic transporting people from all over the world to her docks, was a breeding ground for all types of diseases. A sailor might come off a ship ill to die a short time later, and to be buried in the sands far away from his home port. It is, therefore, no surprise that Provincetown has a number of smallpox graves, unmarked, identity unknown. Here they rest forgotten in the moors of what is now the Cape Cod National Seashore.

Nowadays, smallpox has been wiped from the globe. All that remain are the lonely stones here and there in remote spots, their chiseled words calling across the centuries – "Died with the smallpox."

Truro's Tower of Love

Sitting on a lonely bluff just south of Highland Light in North Truro is the so-called Jenny Lind Tower. Most tourists know nothing about the structure and few Cape Codders have ever visited it.

More than fifty-five feet high, the granite tower looks something like a miniature Provincetown Monument. But that was not the inspiration for that structure. Originally part of the Fitchburg Railroad Depot building in Boston, the tower was purchased and moved to its present location in 1927 by Boston attorney Harry M. Aldrich.

There are two stories as to why the tower came to be where it is. The first is that Mr. Aldrich's grandfather was an official with the Boston and Maine Railroad that had originally built the depot. It is thought by some that Mr. Aldrich wanted a suitable memorial for his grandfather and chose to move one of the four turrets to a piece of land that he owned in Truro.

The second and certainly more romantic tale revolves around the personality of Jenny Lind, the nineteenth-century European singer known as the "Swedish Nightingale," and Mr. Aldrich's admiration for her.

In the 1850s, shortly after the tower was built, Ms. Lind reportedly sang from the tower to a Boston crowd during an East Coast tour. Mr. Aldrich was almost certainly too young to have been personally in attendance at Ms. Lind's performance, but the story is that he was apparently so taken by accounts of the Scandinavian singer's beauty that he carried a life-long torch for her. He read everything about her he could get his hands on and saved any memorabilia that celebrated her career. His infatuation with the diva led to the reason Jenny Lind

Jenny Lind Tower of the Truro Highlands. Jim Coogan Collection

has a connection with Cape Cod.

When the depot was being torn down in 1927, Aldrich brought the tower to the Cape in sections by railroad car and had it re-built, stone by numbered stone, in North Truro as a personal tribute to Ms. Lind. It took five men more than two months to reassemble the tower.

Whether Mr. Aldrich ever visited his completed monument is lost to the memory of those who live in Truro today. Few people make the walk to it anymore. It is now the home of pigeons, owls and white-tailed deer. The late Tom Kane, who knew as much about Truro history as just about anyone (and who also appreciated a good story), said that on moonlit nights when the wind is just right it is possible to hear the voice of the soprano coming from the direction of the tower.

A Cape Codder's Gift to Japan.

When it comes to photography, Japan ranks as a world leader. What is not widely known is that Japan's success in developing a first rate photography industry stems, at least in part, from a Barnstable man's gift of a camera to one of the country's earliest pioneer photographers.

John Wilson was born in Albany, New York in 1816. For much of his young life Wilson was a sailor. At some point he landed in Barnstable, possibly arriving at the Cape's official point of entry after a long voyage. He met local girl Sarah Bourne and at age 29 married her and settled down in Barnstable village. For the next twenty years Wilson was officially listed as a town resident although he probably spent less than five years at his adopted home. As Henry David Thoreau would have described such an individual's connection to Cape Cod, John Wilson was "lightly salted."

Still, when Wilson left Barnstable to go to Japan in the fall of 1860 his passport application had him as a Barnstable resident. No one is sure how Wilson learned the art of photography. The industry was still in its infancy and was practically unknown in Japan. Arriving in Yokohama, Wilson joined a group of German photographers engaged in a pictorial survey of what was still very much an unknown land. Open to outsiders for less than ten years, the Empire of the Sun was of great curiosity to Westerners and the Prussian East Asian Expedition was one of the first to produce views of the country. Wilson worked with them for several months and was evaluated by his employers as a steady and reliable photographer. Working alongside Wilson was a young Japanese man, Renjo Shimooka.

Shimooka (1823-1914) was the son of a shipping agent to the ruling Tokugawa family. At an early age he showed artistic promise. He wanted desperately to learn the craft of photography but he had no equipment nor was he able to obtain any focused training. During the fifteen months Wilson lived in Yokohama, the Barnstable man appears to have provided at least some rudimentary instruction to Shimooka. But the key to Shimooka's eventual success as the first commercial photographer in Japan was the gift of a camera and some chemicals given to him by John Wilson. Wilson traded the camera for Shimooka's work on a 900-foot painted panorama showing scenes of traditional Japanese life. Wilson planned to exhibit the work for profit in London later that year. When Wilson left Japan in January of 1862, he had the panorama and Shimooka had the camera—one of perhaps the first half dozen cameras in the entire country.

After much trial and error Shimooka eventually mastered the technical side of photography. By 1865 he was beginning a successful career as a commercial photographer, in time becoming one of the greatest names in the art of photography in Japan. He is often referred to as Japan's "original photographer." As for John Wilson, he made and lost several fortunes, returning for short periods to Barnstable. He ended his life as he had begun it, as a sailor. On a voyage to the Chincha Islands off Peru while his ship was loading a cargo of guano, Wilson caught Yellow Fever and died there in 1868. His family is buried in the Cobb's Hill Cemetery, but John Wilson rests alone and forgotten on a small Pacific island.

Marconi Cape Cod & the Titanic

The eastern coastline of Wellfleet greets the realm and majesty of the sea, the titanic roar of the Atlantic Ocean's crashing waves spilling the earth's energy upon the sands. Here in this galaxy of sand and sky and sea is the eroding site of the Marconi wireless station, also known as the South Wellfleet wireless transmitting station. On January 19, 1903 this station sent a message from President Theodore Roosevelt to Edward VII, King of England, making it the site of the first transatlantic message sent from the United States.

The first actual transatlantic signal, which consisted of merely the letter "S," was sent from England to Newfoundland in December 1901, the year before the Wellfleet station was completed. During 1902, the first full message spanned the Atlantic, sent from England and received at Nova Scotia. Shortly thereafter the Roosevelt to Edward VII message was sent from Wellfleet. This historic message had its beginnings a quarter century earlier with the birth of Italian inven-

From this site in South Wellfleet, Guglielmo Marconi sent the first transatlantic wireless message. Source: H.A. Dickerman & Son, Taunton, Massachusetts. Jim Coogan collection.

tor Guglielmo Marconi at Bologna on April 25, 1874. By age sixteen Marconi was experimenting at home on wireless modes of telegraphy and was actually successful in sending signals short distances across his backyard. In 1895, at the age of twenty-one, he transmitted a signal one mile. Four years later he successfully sent messages over a span of twenty miles from ship to shore. Next he spanned the English Channel. And in 1901, the Atlantic Ocean.

Construction on the Wellfleet station began in 1901, but a storm destroyed the towers and the station had to be rebuilt. Larger towers were erected – four of them, each two hundred and ten feet high – to support the antenna network. They were constructed of three-inch by twelve-inch lumber and stood on concrete bases, twelve one-inch steel cables supporting each against the Atlantic winds. The transmitter house contained a 20,000 volt condenser, the antenna tuning coil, and the whirling sparkgap rotor that could be heard four miles away. The power station housed a 45-horsepower generator that supplied 2,200 volts AC, increased to the 20,000 volts necessary to spark the airwaves, with a transmitting range of between 1,600 and 3,500 miles.

Besides the January 1903 message to Edward VII, the station played a role in another historic event that linked the British and the

Remnants of the Marconi Wireless Station upon an eroding cliff in Wellfleet.
Photo: Jack Sheedy

Americans. Just after midnight on April 15, 1912, the Wellfleet station received a distress call from the sinking White Star liner *RMS Titanic*. Earlier that evening, the station was busy relaying messages across the crisp, star-filled night air to the station at Cape Race on Newfoundland, messages from family and friends of *Titanic* passengers, passed on from New York, as the liner approached North America on her well-publicized maiden voyage.

Also monitoring and perhaps preparing to pass on some of these messages was radio operator Harold Cottam of the *Carpathia*, of the Cunard line. *Carpathia* was about 58 miles southeast and unaware of the disaster when Cottam sent the following message to the *Titanic* at 12:25 am: *"I say, old man, do you know there is a batch of messages coming through for you from MCC?"* The "MCC" refers to the Cape Cod station at Wellfleet – Marconi Cape Cod.

Titanic's senior radio operator, Jack Phillips, then sent back the following reply: *"Come at once. We have struck a berg. It's a CQD (Come Quick, Danger), old man. Position 41.46 N 50.14W."* Just two hours later the magnificent White Star Liner would be resting on the ocean floor, two and a half miles below the surface, taking 1,500 souls with her.

A placard at the Marconi site mentions that MCC did receive a distress call from the *Titanic*. That message could have been received directly from the *Titanic*, or else was passed on to the Cape Cod station from a ship at sea on that night – either the *Carpathia*, *Frankfort*, or *Mount Temple* – or perhaps even from Cape Race station. These messages would then have been forwarded on from Cape Cod to New York, thus informing the world of the drama unfolding aboard the "unsinkable" liner. In that sense, the quiet town of Wellfleet played a role in the greatest ship disaster of all time.

As the United States entered World War I the Wellfleet station was closed. The four massive towers were dismantled and the buildings were abandoned to the elements and the eroding cliff. During the Kennedy administration the site was acquired by the National Park Service and made a permanent exhibit. At the site are some remnants – timbers and bricks – but over the past century the eroding cliff has devoured more than half the land upon which the station once sat.

Lost Deeds, Indeed

On the breezy evening of October 22, 1827 the regulars shuffled into Crocker Tavern along the main route in Barnstable Village. According to Josiah Hinckley, one of a handful of men playing cards at the tavern that evening, it was "blowing almost a gale." With Hinckley was Joseph Bursley. Little did they know that their card game would be interrupted by an event that would impact the residents of Barnstable County for centuries to come.

Across the road stood the County House, home to the Registry of Deeds, as well as the Clerk of Courts and the Probate Office. These offices held irreplaceable records dating back to the time of settlement. Near 11:00 p.m., with the card game still in progress, "the knocker of the front door was put into rapid motions, attended with the cry of fire," according to Hinckley as documented in Donald Trayser's book, *Barnstable: Three Centuries of a Cape Cod Town*.

Reverend Henry Hersey of the east parish had noticed flames coming from the County House. Hinckley and Bursley sprang into action, and assisted by Reverend Hersey and Isaac Chipman, entered the building through the front door and passed probate records out an open window. Attempts to reach other parts of the building, such as the Registry of Deeds on the second floor, were hampered by thick smoke. So they decided to make another attempt from outside using a ladder. Hinckley climbed to the window where he kicked in the glass and managed to save one volume of deeds before escaping the growing flames. Ninety-three volumes were lost, destroying land records centuries old. Such a devastating loss of information and local history has forever left a void in Barnstable's past and has raised questions over past property ownership, and it is why a majority of land deeds on Cape Cod are of the quitclaim variety.

"Witchmere" Harbor

Though today the horse tracks are long gone, remembered only by telltale street names in some towns, during the latter half of the 19th century horse racing was a popular form of entertainment on Cape Cod for anyone with a taste for the track and some money to wager. Tracks could be found in a number of locations, such as West Dennis where the half-mile Riverside Trotting Park rested near the banks of Swan River, in the vicinity of the appropriately-named Trotting Park Road, with grandstands which held more than two hundred spectators, a judge's stand, and a water tank for the horses. Admission was twenty-five cents.

According to Donald Trayser's *Barnstable: Three Centuries of a Cape Cod Town*, "Nearly all villages of Barnstable had their trotting parks," including the Hyannis Trotting Park and the Barnstable Fairgrounds located at the Agricultural Hall, the site of the county fair. Falmouth had a track off Gifford Street that attracted one thousand spectators on race day, with purses that ran into thousands of dollars.

Harwichport had a racetrack which ran around a circular pond near Nantucket Sound. According to New England historian Edward Rowe Snow, in his book *A Pilgrim Returns to Cape Cod*, "It was the custom for the old sea captains to race their horses around this fresh water pond in Harwichport, and there were many thrilling encounters in which as much as fifty bushels of oats was the gambling stake." Snow's account includes the opinion of local ladies who considered the events that went on there as "devilish" in nature. In addition to the racing and gambling and other tomfoolery, there was a hotel nearby in which "activities of various and sundry nature were said to have taken place." The hotel eventually burned and interest in horseracing waned. Eventually, a cut was made from the pond to Nantucket Sound creating a harbor, today known as Wychmere Harbor, although Snow claims that it was once known as "Witchmere" Harbor, perhaps for the "wicked" activities that went on there.

Helen Keller's Cape Cod Connection

In her autobiography, *The Story of My Life*, Helen Keller tells of her first experience with swimming in salt water on Cape Cod. "I thrust out my hands to grab some support and clutched at the water and at the seaweed which the waves tossed in my face. But all my frantic efforts were in vain. The waves seemed to be playing a game with me and tossed me from one to another in their wild frolic. It was fearful." Miss Keller eventually overcame her fears and, over the course of a number of visits to the beach, became quite comfortable in the arms of the sea. By the end of her first summer, she had learned to float and to go into deep water. She even brought a horseshoe crab home to the house where she was staying, thinking that by keeping it in the well it might make an unusual playmate.

How this young girl, who later became so famous as a person who transcended severe childhood disabilities, came to the New England seacoast from her native Alabama can be traced to a Brewster woman and the widow of Cape Cod sea captain.

Sophia Crocker married Captain Charles Hopkins in January of 1860 at the Unitarian Church in Brewster. As was the case with many wives of sea captains, Sophia didn't see a lot of her husband because of his voyages to various parts of the world. In 1866, while in command of the brig *Lorana*, Captain Hopkins was stricken with a fever and died in Havana, Cuba. In addition to Sophia, the captain left a daughter that he had never seen.

Sophia Hopkins never re-married and was content to continue living in Brewster at the hip-roofed family homestead on Main Street that she eventually named "Kinslow." Apparently she was also comfortable enough financially to be able to winter in Florida. But tragedy struck in 1883 when Sophia's daughter, Florence, died at age sixteen. Perhaps in a need to compensate for the loss of her only child, Sophia took a position at the Perkins Institute for the Blind in South Boston.

There she became a house mother for a number of young girls who were students at the school.

One of the girls in Sophia's charge at Perkins was Annie Sullivan. There was an instant bonding between the two and Annie was invited to summer in Brewster in 1884. Several subsequent summers found Annie Sullivan at Kinslow with Sophia during parts of July and August. Often Sophia let Annie wear some of her daughter's clothes and took her to social events in Brewster. For the poor Irish orphan, the annual summer escape to Brewster must have seemed like a fairy tale.

It was during the summer of 1886 while at Kinslow, following her graduation from Perkins, that Annie received the offer to travel to Tuscumbia, Alabama to teach Helen Keller, a blind and deaf seven-year old. With encouragement from Sophia and the price of a train ticket south provided by her benefactor, Annie left in early 1887 after a short winter visit to Brewster where she and Sophia stayed with Sophia's brother, Thomas Crocker. That year would begin her career as a teacher to one of the more important figures in American history.

What we know of the earliest experiences of Annie Sullivan with the young Helen is largely due to the letters that Annie sent to Sophia Hopkins. The two wrote to each other every week and in an April 1887 letter, Annie told Sophia about the breakthrough she had made with Helen, solving the mystery of language with the connection of the word "water" with the Keller family well pump. These edited letters, which are featured in Helen's autobiography, are especially important as Helen could not recall how she learned language.

The rapid advancements in Helen's first year of education took the child from a deaf mute to an energetic pupil who was beginning to investigate the classics. When Annie and Helen, accompanied by Helen's mother, Kate, came north to visit the Perkins school in 1888, Sophia invited all of them to Kinslow where they spent parts of the summer. This is where Helen was introduced to the beach. For the next eight years, Annie and Helen spent time at Kinslow, using the house as if it were their own if Sophia was away. As for Sophia, on several occasions she was a guest in the Keller home in Alabama and was treated as family.

Sophia Crocker Hopkins died in 1917. Helen, by then a world famous personality, continued to visit the Cape occasionally. She was mentioned as making an automobile trip here in August of 1920. She had moved on to the wider world. But it is interesting to think that in some of the most formative years in Helen Keller's life, it was the town of Brewster, and the caring nurturing of a widowed wife of a Cape Cod sea captain, that had much to do with what this amazing woman would eventually become.

Chapter 9

Dark Secrets

Cape Cod is a peninsula rich in history, yet also rich in mystery. Though representing the outermost reaches of a New World settled by Europeans looking for a fresh start in a new land, this area's settlers certainly brought along enough Old World beliefs and prejudices as part of their baggage. As a result, Cape Cod had its scapegoats – in the form of "witches" Liza Tower Hill and Goody Hallet – who, it was said, cavorted with the Devil. And the Cape had its tales of romance and revenge as well. It all points to a dark side to this "narrow land."

Remembering Barnabas

A landscape of windswept moors marks the lower Cape's eastern shoreline with hillocks sculpted and trees twisted by salt spray breezes. Tales centuries old become sprinkled with a tablespoon of history and a teaspoon of lore in this realm where sky and sand connect with the sea. Such tales may be found in the local folklore volume, *The Narrow Land*, written by Elizabeth Reynard. Within its pages is the tale of a "young theologian" named Barnabas, a Harvard graduate who, with his beautiful wife, Remember, arrived at Nauset in the early 18th century. Apparently the local pastor was getting up in years and it was planned that this young minister would be his replacement. Yet, powerful forces were to make themselves known.

This is the point in the story when history and folklore become intermingled. Remember owned a fiddle – a fiddle that would lead to mischief and eventually, to murder. In fact, according to Reynard, "Never a psalm tune slipped along the bright strings of the fiddle."

One day as Barnabas returned home after ministering to the ill he could hear a fiddle playing. He approached the house, and as he looked in a window he discovered his new bride dancing to a tune fiddled by a sailor. But when Barnabas burst through the door Remember was alone.

That evening Barnabas broke the devilish fiddle into small pieces.

Yet, stranger still becomes the tale. A number of times, while returning home from ministering, Barnabas could have sworn he heard the fiddle playing. According to *The Narrow Land*, the minister said, "Wife, give to me that Instrument of Satan," to which his wife responded, "'Tis only the sin that sings in thy soul."

So troublesome became the phantom fiddling that Barnabas had a new house built with bars installed over the windows, making Remember a prisoner in her own home where she was confined for a period of three years. Regardless, Barnabas continued to hear fiddle playing when he returned home at the end of each day. Yet, when he threw open the door he would find Remember alone in the house, and the fiddle nowhere to be found.

The devilish fiddle haunted and taunted the minister until he reached a breaking point. Convinced of his wife's "evil" ways, in a fit of delirium he murdered her and set the house ablaze. As the building was consumed, the sound of fiddling could be heard above the crackling flames. In either a case of madness or remorse, that evening Barnabas entered Higgins Tavern where he wrote out his confession and then left to drown himself in the aptly-named Minister's Pond.

The Witch of Half Way Pond

Elizabeth Lewis was born on January 17, 1711 to Benjamin Lewis of Barnstable and his second wife, Hannah Hinckley, who was a cousin of Massachusetts Governor Thomas Hinckley. Hannah died when Elizabeth was a child, leaving Benjamin to raise his daughter alone at their home near Crooked Pond located in the wilderness between the villages of Barnstable and Hyannis, two miles from their nearest neighbor.

From the beginning Elizabeth Lewis was considered odd by townsfolk as she did not possess the more feminine qualities of her contemporaries in the populated areas. She can best be described as a

Winged skulls and heads on tombstones were meant to help usher the soul of the deceased to their reward in heaven. Here, three different styles of Cape headstones are represented. Photos: Jack Sheedy.

tomboy, one quite learned in farming and in the ways of the forest. In those days, the forest was known to harbor Natives and wild animals, but to Elizabeth neither was to be feared so long as they were treated with respect. The townsfolk, on the other hand, were not accustomed to such "hostilities" and therefore could not understand Elizabeth's "strange" way of life.

At age seventeen Elizabeth married William Blatchford on November 12, 1728. The couple made a home for themselves near Half Way Pond (now Mary Dunn Pond), one mile west of Benjamin Lewis' house, beside the ancient trail that led from Barnstable to Hyannis. The Blatchfords eventually had eight children, beginning with Peter in 1729 and ending with William in 1750.

Elizabeth was admitted as a member of the East Church of Barnstable while in her mid-20s and was considered "an exemplary member" with only one mishap to mar an otherwise spotless church record. It seems that when her second child died, Thankful Gilbert, a member of the church, charged Elizabeth with abuse. As punishment, Elizabeth was made to read a confession of guilt aloud in public.

William Blatchford was not a religious man and did not accompany his wife to service, only being admitted as a member of the church the day before his death, which came on June 15, 1755, leaving Elizabeth alone to raise her children. To earn a living, she spun, wove, cared for sick animals, and farmed. Hardworking, she was described by Amos Otis in his book *Genealogical Notes of Barnstable Families* as "honest, industrious, energetic and shrewd in making a bargain." According to Barnstable town records, in 1773 she was fined for "selling spirituous liquor without a license." She performed hard physical labor into her seventy-fifth year of age, and died in June 1790 at the age of seventy-nine. Elizabeth Blatchford's mortal remains were interred at the cemetery of the East Church, where she was a member.

In eighteenth century New England there was no precedent for an independent woman forging her own life, maintaining a farm, and raising children on her own. Since the townsfolk could not understand her way of life apart from the rest of the population, Elizabeth became a scapegoat and was labeled a witch. And they believed she could not have survived in such a hostile forest setting without some form of assistance, supernatural in nature. It was believed that such assistance came from the Devil himself.

The townsfolk dubbed her Liza Tower Hill, referencing the Tower Hill section of London whence her husband's ancestors hailed. At night, under the moon, it was said that Liza performed a Satanic dance upon the surface of Half Way Pond, bare breasted and with her feet aflame, devilish fish swimming beneath her. Mutant animals appeared on shore around the pond and strange lights shone in the forest as travelers between Barnstable and Hyannis would become bewitched by Liza Tower Hill's spells.

Yet, even after her death in 1790 it was believed her ghost haunted the forest and the pond, continuing to bewitch those who dared travel the dark path by night. There exist a number of stories involving Elizabeth Blatchford's alter ego, Liza Tower Hill – stories of her both as a witch and as a ghost. In fact, a Mr. Wood of West Barnstable brought a formal charge against Elizabeth Blatchford – the only one on record – accusing her of being a witch. He claimed she turned him into a horse and rode him to Plum Pudding Pond in Plymouth in order to attend a Witches' Sabbath. Wood's case was dropped for lack of evidence.

Benjamin Goodspeed of East Sandwich also claimed that the witch Liza Tower Hill would, on occasion, turn him into a horse and ride him all night long over Cape Cod. In an effort to escape her bewitching powers, Goodspeed went to sea, figuring he was safe on board a sailing vessel far from the forest of Barnstable. But the witch followed him in the form of her familiar, a black cat. One evening, according to folklore, the cat swam up to the ship, boarded the vessel, and then transformed itself into Liza Tower Hill. The witch then turned Goodspeed into a horse and rode him throughout the night. The next evening, Goodspeed was ready as the cat swam toward the ship. On the advice of a shipmate, he rolled a wet page from the Bible into a pellet and with a musket shot the cat dead.

Folklore suggests that the witch's ghost haunts two places in the town of Barnstable – the forest wilderness where she lived and the Allyn House in Barnstable. For instance, on Christmas night in 1810 seventy-one-year-old Dr. Richard Bourne was headed home along the old trail after celebrating at a local pub. As he neared Half Way Pond he noticed a burning stump around which danced the ghost of Liza Tower Hill. Bourne, in a fit of holiday merriment, spent the night singing and dancing around the stump with the ghost. Come the next morning he awoke alone.

The Allyn House, built around 1680 and considered one of the Cape's oldest houses, was believed haunted by the ghost of Liza Tower Hill. Even before her death, her familiar was believed to frequent the house to avenge the apparent mistreatment of her daughter, Lydia, who was employed there as a servant. Soon after Lydia was hired strange things began to happen, which were blamed on the witch Liza Tower Hill, and after her death, on her ghost. Clocks and dishes would become smashed, sometimes in the middle of the night. The family was kept awake at night by knocks upon the walls and other ungodly sounds. Six chairs, which were purchased just the day before, were found smashed to bits by invisible hands. And a black cat appeared whenever the servant Lydia was either mistreated or made to do more work than her mother felt she should do.

These folktales have survived for more than two hundred years and will perhaps survive for another two hundred, adding a layer of mystery to Barnstable's rich history. But one should not forget that behind the folklore is the true story of a woman, not a witch, who grew up in the wilderness of eighteenth century Barnstable, married, raised children, died, and was buried as a member of the church.

Love Gone Wrong

Cape Cod is certainly a romantic locale with its long beaches and its picturesque dunes providing plenty of spots to steal a kiss. Yet, not all love stories ended well as these tales of love gone wrong will attest.

The first great Cape Cod romance occurred long ago, before written history, and involved two legendary Native spirits – the giant Maushop and the sea woman Squant, a temptress with seaweed hair and a body of kelp who attempted to lure the unsuspecting Maushop to her watery den with her enchanting song. Maushop, who is best remembered for creating the islands of Nantucket and Martha's Vineyard with sand from his moccasins, was enthralled by the sea woman and longed for her companionship. Though it would seem to be a long-distance romance – after all, Squant lived underwater and Maushop required air to breathe – Maushop eventually visited

The cliffs of Wellfleet, atop which Goodie Hallett cursed Sam Bellamy, sending the pirate and his vessel Whydah to a watery grave. Photo: Jack Sheedy.

the sea woman's den where he promptly fell asleep and where he sleeps to this day.

Some Europeans didn't fare any better. In 1626, the 40-foot ketch, *Sparrow-Hawk*, bound for Virginia with about 25 people aboard, wrecked on Nauset Beach. All hands survived, and with the help of Natives, they made the trip to Plimoth Plantation where they stayed for the winter as guests of the Pilgrims, "sheltered in their houses as well as they could," according to Governor William Bradford's journal. The Governor's journal continues, "The chief amongst these people was one Mr. Fells and Mr. Sibsey, which had many servants belonging unto them, many of them being Irish." After their stay at Plimoth, the *Sparrow-Hawk* passengers left for Virginia, where Mr. Sibsey became a colony councilor. As for Mr. Fells, he was rumored to have had a maidservant at Plimoth whom "he was suspected to keep as his concubine," according to Bradford. Later the maidservant "appeared she was with child," and so the two hightailed it from Plimoth.

Cape Cod's most storied romance was that of the ill-fated love affair involving a witch and a pirate. Maria Hallett did not start off a witch, and Sam Bellamy did not start off a pirate. In fact, their beginnings were quite typical for the early 18th century – Maria was an Eastham girl and Bellamy was an English sailor. The two met, fell in love, and there was talk of marriage, but first Bellamy needed to provide for his future wife. He heard of a fleet of sunken Spanish ships off the Florida coast and planned to recover their riches. So he left Cape Cod, promising to return. Yet, treasure hunting proved fruitless so, desperate, he turned to piracy. Over a short period of time Bellamy captured a number of vessels, including the *Whydah*, and reaped a vast fortune.

Meanwhile, back on Cape Cod, Maria was pregnant with Bellamy's child, which died on the night it was born. Imprisoned and charged with neglect, Maria managed to escape and retreated to the moors of Wellfleet where she scratched out a living. Townsfolk considered her a witch, nicknaming her "Goodie." Ostracized by the townsfolk, she promised to enact revenge upon the man who ruined her. So, when Bellamy revisited these shores aboard the *Whydah*, one stormy night in 1717, the witch "Goodie" Hallett conjured up a wicked tempest that sent the pirate and his ship to their doom.

Not sure if it was love or simply greed, but the story remains of Hannah Screecham, who was known to *befriend* pirates that frequented Grand Island (now known as Oyster Harbors) in the vicinity of Cotuit and West bays. Though she may or may not have been a witch – apparently her sister, Sarah, was a witch – Hannah's activities were certainly dark and mysterious. The tale goes that she would assist pirates looking to bury their treasures on the beach, only to push them into the hole and bury them alive with their booty. Alas, whenever she attempted to dig up the treasures the ghosts of those pirates would rise from their graves and prevent her. To this day, Hannah Screecham's ghost is said to haunt the area, her screeching wails carrying with the wicked wind.

Hell certainly hath no fury like a woman scorned.

The White Witch

Stories abound of ships and of sea captains considered cursed, as if Poseidon himself held a personal grudge. Some Cape shipmasters wrecked two or even three vessels over the course of their seafaring career and were eventually told to inquire inland for future employment. Were they cursed souls? Or just bad mariners? Perhaps it was a combination of both.

One well respected Cape Cod sea captain was Centerville's Josiah Richardson. Over the course of a 32-year career he eventually became one of the country's premier shipmasters and in May 1852 was rewarded with the command of the new 240-foot clipper ship *Staffordshire*. Well-appointed to accommodate oceangoing passengers in the greatest level of comfort and luxury available, she was among the greatest vessels afloat in her day, with artistic woodwork decorating her stern depicting an English scene on one side and an American scene on the other. Yet, doom awaited the *Staffordshire* between these two sides of the Atlantic.

Bad omens appeared to haunt the ship right from the beginning, prompted it seems by the fact that the *Staffordshire* had a figurehead in the form of a white witch at her bow. Sisters Margaret and Catherine Fox of Arcadia, New York, who were famous mediums of the day, announced that the figurehead would spell disaster for the vessel, her crew, and her passengers. The Fox sisters, who had helped to bring about the American spiritual movement in 1848 when they reported hearing rapping noises on the walls in their home, had a large and devoted legion of followers, said to be about one million strong by the mid-1850s. So, when they spoke, many people listened. In fact, so widespread became their predictions of doom for the *Staffordshire* that the ship's departure from Boston was delayed. Captain Richardson and his new vessel were eventually on their way, departing on May 3, 1852 and arriving safely at San Francisco, concluding a 101-day voyage which broke a number of speed records along the way.

Next, Richardson took his new command across the Pacific to India, breaking more records including a speedy 83-day passage home from Calcutta to Boston. Richardson might have made the journey one day shorter had he braved some nasty weather as he approached the New England coast. With a shipload of passengers he took the safer option and reduced speed in order to avoid trouble, proving that he was a sea captain for all seasons, speedy yet cautious and always accommodating.

Later in 1853, Richardson sailed the *Staffordshire* across the Atlantic to Liverpool. His letters to his wife during November and December pose occasional dark reflections as the steady and skilled shipmaster seemed to possess misgivings about his upcoming journey home. His letters appear filled with premonitions of disaster:

November 11: "Should much prefer selling the ship and returning home in steamer … many accidents have occurred to the best ships and the most able commanders."

November 18: "Wish I was with you and did not have to make the western passage."

December 5: "In case of any accident to me, this will show how my account stands with (the *Staffordshire's* owners) … Life is uncertain, we both know, and all the property I possess I wish my dear wife and children to have and enjoy."

That December, the *Staffordshire* left Liverpool on her western passage with nearly 200 passengers and crew, and "the greatest amount of freight on board ever taken from Liverpool to Boston," according to Richardson. About two weeks at sea, on December 23, a fierce storm damaged the rudder-head. Additional damage during a gale on the 28th took away "the bowsprit, foretopmast, fore yard and everything forward," according to the testimony of First Mate Joseph Alden. Captain Richardson went aloft to assess the damage and fell to the deck below, severely damaging his back. He was transferred to his cabin where he was attended by the ship's surgeon. From his cot the captain of the *Staffordshire* continued to give orders to Alden, but conditions worsened.

Another storm hit the ship on the 29th, the wind growing into a hurricane, according to Alden. Around midnight, the *Staffordshire* struck rocks near Sable Island, south of Nova Scotia and as she drifted away from the rocks she began to settle as water flooded inside. Initially, Alden considered grounding the vessel, but with limited maneuverability and a crew in disorder, the thought was dashed. Pumps could not keep pace – fourteen inches of water in her hold quickly grew to four feet over the course of ten minutes. It became apparent, the ship would not survive. So, efforts commenced toward saving the passengers and crew.

Richardson, unable to leave his cot, realized his earlier feelings of dread had come true. There was one last hope. He estimated the water near Sable Island was shallow enough that the vessel's hull would hit bottom before she submerged completely. Alden informed his captain that, unfortunately, the ship had drifted into deeper waters and would sink. He then offered to carry Richardson to a lifeboat. The captain declined, reportedly saying, "Then I am lost, God's will be done," and he went down with his ship along with some 175 others in what was one of the most tragic passenger wrecks of the nineteenth century.

Believers in such things will say the *Staffordshire* was cursed from the beginning, for she tempted Fate by carrying a figurehead in the form of a white witch. It is of interest to note that the vessel met her doom at midnight – the witching hour. Perhaps the Fox sisters were right all along.

Eugene O'Neill's Revenge on a Provincetown Librarian

Pulitzer Prize-winning playwright Eugene O'Neill was known for modeling characters in his plays after people from his own life. The casting could be thinly veiled, or it could be obvious. Often these characters were tributes to lost comrades, such as when he modeled Joe Mott in *The Iceman Cometh* after his friend, Joe Smith, a black New York City gambler. He even used members of his own family as models as in the case of his wayward son, Shane, as the doomed Don Parritt in *The Iceman Cometh*. But what he did to a Provincetown librarian proved that he could be a cruel and vindictive man.

Abbie Putnam ran the Provincetown library during the days when O'Neill and his entourage of Greenwich Village friends summered in the east end. She was an eccentric and legendary personality in Provincetown. O'Neill's first dust up with this middle-aged spinster was in the late winter of 1917 when he'd come to the Cape tip by himself to do some writing. Putnam regarded herself as the supreme guardian of the book collection and was very particular about who had access to it. Still relatively unknown as a writer and a "stranger" in a close-knit year-round community, O'Neill got no special treatment from Miss Putnam. He didn't qualify for a library card because he was not a property owner and he was required to have someone local sign for him. She was hard of hearing and he spoke softly, which further complicated their relationship. As O'Neill sat in the reading room Putnam watched him closely and she restricted the number of books that he was allowed to take out. O'Neill chaffed at the scrutiny and what he saw as the priggish way she controlled her domain. During that winter and spring, O'Neill drafted a play set in a coastal town that featured a deaf librarian with a homely face. It was never produced. In the next two years, the antagonism between the librarian and the playwright grew to the point where Miss Putnam actually threw O'Neill out of the library one time when he showed up loud and drunk. The fact that O'Neill had just won the Pulitzer Prize, for *Beyond the Horizon,* made no difference to Abbie Putnam. Whenever O'Neill attempted to use the library he found Abbie Putnam as an uncooperative adversary.

When O'Neill wrote *Desire Under the Elms* in 1923, he hadn't forgotten the perceived slights that he'd received from Abbie Putnam. The play featured a woman, married to an older man, who seduces her stepson and then, after becoming pregnant, eventually ends up killing her baby. Some psychologists have interpreted the play as a sort of unconscious autobiography centering on O'Neill's recent loss of his mother. A New York critic said of *Desire,* "Mr. O'Neill's dramas always make me glad that I am not one of the characters involved." But in this dark tragedy, Eugene O'Neill included a person from his Provincetown experience in the character of the adulteress and baby killer. And the flawed and tragic character? – Abbie Putnam. He never even changed her name! O'Neill had gotten his revenge on the Cape Cod librarian who had once denied him a library card.

BIBLIOGRAPHY

Arber, Edward. The Story of the Pilgrim Fathers, 1606-1623 A.D., As Told by Themselves, Their Friends, and Their Enemies. London: Houghton, Mifflin & Co., 1897.

Archer, Gabriel. Gosnold's Settlement at Cuttyhunk. Boston, MA. Directors of the Old South Work, Boston, MA, 1896.

Archer, Gleason L. With Axe and Musket at Plymouth. New York, NY: The American Historical Society, Inc, 1936.

Barnard, Ruth L. A History of Orleans. Taunton, MA: William S. Sullwold Publishing, 1975.

Barbour, Harriot Buxton. Sandwich – The Town That Glass Built. Boston, MA: Houghton Mifflin Co., 1948.

Barnstable County. Three Centuries of a Cape Cod County: Barnstable, Massachusetts, 1685-1985. Barnstable, MA: Barnstable County, 1985.

Bingham, Amelia. Mashpee: Land of the Wampanoags. Mashpee, MA: Mashpee Centennial Committee, 1970.

Bodensiek, Fred. Barnstable at 350. Barnstable, MA: Barnstable 350th Committee, 1989.

Bowles, Francis Tiffany. The Loyalty of Barnstable in the Revolution. Reprinted from the publications of the Colonial Society of Massachusetts, Vol. XXV. Cambridge, MA: John Wilson & Son, The University Press, 1924.

Bradford, William. Bradford's History of Plymouth Plantation. Boston, MA: Wright & Potter Printing Co, 1898.

Bray, Mary Mathews. A Sea Trip in Clipper Ship Days. Boston, MA: Badger, 1920

Brigham, Albert Perry. Cape Cod and the Old Colony. New York, NY: Grosset & Dunlap, 1920.

Cabral, Reginald W. Wooden Ships and Iron Men. Provincetown, MA: Trustees of the Provincetown Heritage Museum, 1994.

Carpenter, Delores Bird. Early Encounters: Native Americans and Europeans in New England. From the papers of W. Sears Nickerson. East Lansing, MI: Michigan State University Press, 1994.

Cataldo, Louis. Pictorial Tales of Cape Cod. Hyannis, MA: Tales of Cape Cod, Inc, 1956.

Chatham, Dennis & Marion. Cape Coddities. Boston, MA & New York, NY: Houghton Mifflin Co, 1920.

Clark, Admont G. Lighthouses of Cape Cod, Martha's Vineyard, Nantucket. East Orleans, MA: Parnassus Imprint, 1992.

Clark, Admont G. They Built Clipper Ships in Their Back Yard. Yarmouthport, MA: Parnassus Imprint, 1963.

Corbett, Scott. Cape Cod's Way. New York, NY: Thomas Y. Crowell Company, 1955.

Corbett, Scott. The Sea Fox. New York, NY: Thomas Y. Crowell Company, 1956.

Crosby, Katharine. Blue-Water Men & Other Cape Codders. New York, NY: The Macmillan Company, 1946.

Cullity, Rosanna and John Nye. A Sandwich Album. Sandwich, MA: Nye Family of America Society, 1987.

Dalton, J.W. The Lifesavers of Cape Cod. Chatham, MA: The Chatham Press, Inc., 1967

Depauw, Linda Grant. Seafaring Women. Boston, MA: Houghton-Mifflin Co., 1982.

Deyo, Simeon L. History of Barnstable County, Massachusetts 1620-1890. New York, NY: H.W. Blake & Co, 1890.

Digges, Jeremiah (Josef Berger). Cape Cod Pilot. Provincetown, MA & New York, NY: Modern Pilgrim Press and Viking Press, 1937.

Doane, Doris. Exploring Old Cape Cod. Chatham, MA: The Chatham Press, Inc., 1968.

Eastham Tercentenary Committee. Eastham Massachusetts, 1651-1951. Eastham, MA: Eastham Tercentenary Committee, 1951.

Eaton, John P. and Charles A. Haas. Titanic – Destination Disaster. New York, NY: W. W. Norton, 1996.

Fawsett, Marise. Cape Cod Annals. Bowie, MD: Heritage Books, Inc., 1990.

Farson, Robert. Cape Cod Railroads: Including Martha's Vineyard and Nantucket.Yarmouth Port, MA: Cape Cod Historical Publications, 1990.

Farson, Robert. The Cape Cod Canal. Middletown, CT: Wesleyan University Press, 1977.

Freeman, Frederick. The History of Cape Cod. Yarmouth Port, MA: Parnassus Imprints, 1965.

Gamble, Adam. 1880 Atlas of Barnstable County. Yarmouthport, MA: On Cape Publications, 1998.

Giambarba, Paul. Surfmen and Lifesavers. Centerville, MA: Scrimshaw Publishing, 1967.

Giambarba, Paul. The Picture Story of Cape Cod. Centerville, MA: The Scrimshaw Press: 1965.

Gibson, Marjorie Hubbell. Historical & Genealogical Atlas and Guide to Barnstable County. Teaticket, MA: Falmouth Genealogical Society, 1995.

Gibson, Marjorie Hubbell. H.M.S. Somerset: 1746-1778. Cotuit, MA: Abbey Gate House, 1992.

Green, Eugene and William Sachse. Names of the Land. Chester, CT: Globe Pequot Press, 1983.

Holly, H.H. Sparrow-hawk: A Seventeenth Century Vessel in Twentieth Century America. Boston, MA: The Nimrod Press, 1969.

Hurd, Edith Thacher. The Wreck of the Wild Wave: Being the True Account of the Clipper Ship Wild Wave of Boston. New York, NY: Oxford University Press, 1942.

Inquirer & Mirror. A Brief History of Nantucket's 300 Years. Nantucket, MA, 1959.

Ivanoff, Josephine Buck. Pieces of Old Cape Cod. Jack Claire Viall, 1985.

Jalbert, Russell R. Where Sea & History Meet – 4000 Years of Life in Orleans. Orleans, MA: Orleans Bicentennial Commission, 1997.

Janes, Edward C. When Cape Cod Men Saved Lives. Champaign, IL: Garrard Publishing Co., 1968.

Johnson, Jack. Stories of Cape Cod. Plymouth, MA: Memorial Press of Plymouth, 1944.

Kane, Tom. My Pamet. Mount Kisco, NY: Moyer Bell Limited, 1989.

Keene, Betsey D. History of Bourne from 1622 to 1937. Yarmouthport, MA: Charles W. Swift, 1937.

King, H. Roger. Cape Cod & Plymouth Colony in the Seventeenth Century. Lanham, MD: University Press of America, 1994.

Kittredge, Henry C. Cape Cod: Its People & Their History. Boston, MA: Houghton Mifflin Company, 1968.

Kittredge, Henry C. Mooncussers of Cape Cod. New York, NY: Houghton Mifflin Co., 1937.

Kittredge, Henry C. Shipmasters of Cape Cod. Boston, MA & New York, NY: Houghton Mifflin Company, 1935.

Knowles, Katharine. Cape Cod Journey. Barre, MA: Barre Publishers, 1966.

Lawson, Evelyn. Yesterday's Cape Cod. Miami, FL: E.A. Seemann Publishing, Inc., 1975.

Leighton, Clare. Where Land Meets Sea. Chatham, MA: The Chatham Press, Inc., 1973.

Lincoln, Joseph C. Cape Cod Yesterdays. New York, NY: Blue Ribbon Books, 1939.

Lord, Walter. A Night to Remember. New York, NY: Bantam Books, 1955.

Lombard Jr., Asa Cobb Paine. East of Cape Cod. New Bedford, MA: Reynolds-De Walt Printing, Inc, 1976.

Lovell, Jr., R.A. Sandwich – A Cape Cod Town. Sandwich, MA : Town of Sandwich Archives & Historical Center, 1984.

Lowe, Alice A. Nauset on Cape Cod – A History of Eastham. Eastham, MA: Eastham Historical Society, 1968.

Neal, Allan. Cape Cod is a Number of Things. Yarmouth Port, MA: The Register Press, 1954.

Oldale, Robert N. Cape Cod and the Islands: The Geologic Story. East Orleans, MA: Parnassus Imprint, 1992.

O'Neil, Neva. Master Mariners of Dennis. Dennis, MA: Dennis Historical Society, 1965.

Orleans Historical Society. Rescue CG36500. Orleans, MA: Lower Cape Publishing, 1985.

Otis, Amos. Genealogical Notes of Barnstable Families. Barnstable, MA: F.B. & F.P. Goss Publishers and Printers, 1888.

Pohl, Frederick J. The Vikings on Cape Cod. Pictou, Nova Scotia: Pictou Advocate Press, 1957.

Quinn, William. Cape Cod Maritime Disasters. Orleans, MA: Lower Cape Publishing, 1990.

Quinn, William P. Shipwrecks Around Cape Cod. Orleans, MA: Lower Cape Publishing, 1973.

Quinn, William P. The Saltworks of Historic Cape Cod. Orleans, MA: Parnassus Imprint, 1993.

Reid, Nancy Thacher. Dennis, Cape Cod. Dennis, MA: Dennis Historical Society, 1996.

Reid, William James. The Building of the Cape Cod Canal. Privately printed, 1961.

Reynard, Elizabeth. The Narrow Land. Chatham, MA: Chatham Historical Society, 1978.

Ryder, Marion Crowell. Cape Cod Remembrances. Taunton, MA: William S. Sullwold Publishing, 1972.

Small, Isaac M. Shipwrecks on Cape Cod. Chatham, MA: The Chatham Press, Inc., 1967.

Smith, Mary Lou. The Book of Falmouth: A Tercentennial Celebration 1686-1986. Falmouth, MA: Falmouth Historical Society, 1986.

Smith, Mary Lou. Woods Hole Reflections. Woods Hole, MA: Woods Hole Historical Society, 1983.

Smith, William C. A History of Chatham, Massachusetts. Chatham, MA: Chatham Historical Society, 1971.

Snow, Edward Rowe. A Pilgrim Returns to Cape Cod. Boston, MA: The Yankee Publishing Co., 1946.

Snow, Edward Rowe. New England Sea Tragedies: New York, NY: Dodd, Mead & Co., 1960.

Snow, Edward Rowe. The Lighthouses of New England. New York, NY: Dodd, Mead & Co., 1945

Swift, Charles F. Cape Cod. Yarmouthport, MA: Register Publishing Company, 1897.

Swift, Charles F. History of Old Yarmouth. Yarmouthport, MA: The Historical Society of Old Yarmouth, 1975.

Tarbell, Arthur Wilson. Cape Cod Ahoy. Boston, MA: A.T. Ramsay and Co, 1932.

Thompson, Frederic L. The Lightships of Cape Cod. Portland, ME: Congress Square Press, 1983.

Thoreau, Henry David. Cape Cod. New York, NY: Bramhall House, 1951.

Town of Barnstable. The Seven Villages of Barnstable. Barnstable, MA: Town of Barnstable, 1976.

Trayser, Donald G. Barnstable: Three Centuries of a Cape Cod Town. Hyannis, MA: F.B. & F.P. Goss, 1939.

Various. About Cape Cod. Boston, MA: Thomas Todd Company, 1936.

Vuilleumier, Marion. Cape Cod – A Pictorial History. Norfolk, VA: The Donning Co., 1982.

Vuilleumier, Marion. Earning a Living on Olde Cape Cod. Craigville, MA: Craigville Press, 1968.

Vuilleumier, Marion. The Town of Yarmouth, Massachusetts – A History: 1639-1989. Yarmouth, MA: The Historical Society of Old Yarmouth, 1989.

Wilson, Harold C. Gosnold's Hope: The Story of Bartholomew Gosnold. Greenboro, NC: Tudor Publishers, 2000.

Willison, George P. Saints & Strangers. New York, NY: Time, Inc., 1964.

Webber, Bernard C. Chatham "The Lifeboatmen." Orleans, MA. Lower Cape Publishing Co., 1985.

Whiting, Emma Mayhew & Henry Beetle Hough. Whaling Wives. Boston, MA: Houghton-Mifflin Co., 1953.

Wood, Donald. Cape Cod – A Guide. Boston, MA: Little, Brown & Co., 1973.

Wood, William. New England's Prospect. Amherst, MA: University of Massachusetts Press, 1977.

ADDITIONAL SOURCES & NOTES

CHAPTER 1: EARLY DAYS

The Realm of the Great Spirit

The Narrow Land, by Elizabeth Reynard, pages 23-61.

Vikings Visit Vinland

The Vikings on Cape Cod, by Frederick J. Pohl, pages 5-46; The Narrow Land, by Elizabeth Reynard, pages 3-20.

Cape's Christopher Columbus

Gosnold's Hope: The Story of Bartholomew Gosnold, by Harold C. Wilson, pages 51-60 and 67-74.

Cape Cod: Its People and Their History by Henry C. Kittredge, pages 13-16.

Martin Pring: A Forgotten Cape Explorer

Historical Journal of Massachusetts Vol. XXVI: Summer 1998 No. 2 "Where did Captain Martin Pring Anchor in New England?" by Richard Whalen. Pages 111-123.

"Martin Pring at Provincetown in 1603?" by Warner F. Gookin and David B. Quinn. Published in the New England Quarterly XL (March 1967) pages 79-91.

A Pointed Rear Guard

Samuel de Champlain: Father of New France, Samuel Eliot, Morison, Little, Brown and Company, Boston, MA, page 83.

Cape Cod: Its People and Their History, Henry Kittredge, Houghton Mifflin Company, Boston, MA, 1968, pages 16-18.

CHAPTER 2: AT WORK

Inventive Cape Codders

Cape Cod and all the Pilgrim Land, "Cape Cod Pearls," May 1921.

Cape Cod Mariner, The Journal of the Kittredge Maritime Center, "Native Pearls from herring streams," by James Coogan, Spring 1994.

Great Marshes of West Barnstable

Cape Cod Annals, by Marise Fawsett, page 69-73.

The Glint of Sandwich Glass

www.sandwichglassmuseum.org (and tours at Sandwich Glass Museum, 129 Main Street, Sandwich, MA).

When a Cobb was a Coach

Australian Dictionary of Biography. Vol. 3. 1969 "Freeman Cobb (1830-1878) by K.A. Austin.

"Cobb & Co. – An Australian Transport Icon." www.australia.gov.au/about-autralia/australian-story/cobb-and-co

Obituary: "Death of Hon. Freeman Cobb." Published in the Barnstable Patriot newspaper, July 9, 1878.

H.K Cummings' Telephone Co.

Obituary: Henry Knowles Cummings, published in The Cape Codder, May 21, 1953.

"One Man's Orleans Telephone Company Caused Excitement" The Cape Codder, June 13, 1946.

Italians on Strike

Barnstable Patriot: September 20, 1880, September 25, 1880, November 1, 1880, January 24, 1881, February 7, 1881.

The Building of the Cape Cod Canal, by William James Reid, page 14; The Cape Cod Canal, by Robert Farson, page 21-22

CHAPTER 3: AT SEA

Women Who Went to Sea

Logbook of the New Bedford whaler Gazelle, 1857; Old Dartmouth Historical Society.

Whaling Wives by Emma Mahew Whiting and Henry Beetle Hough, 1953, page 7.

A Sea Trip in Clipper Ship Days by Mary Mathews Bray, 1920.

Logbook of the brig Panama, March 28, 1854; Pilgrim Memorial Museum.

Register, November 21, 1952, page 6.

Hannah Rebecca Crowell Burgess Journals, 1852-1856; Sandwich Historical Society

Cape Cod Life, "Seafaring Women of the 19th Century: Their Encounters with Pirates, Storms and Mutiny," by James and Mary Coogan, Early Summer 1986.

John Adams' Other Abigail

Cape Cod Pilot by Jeremiah Digges, M.I.T. Press, Cambridge, MA, pages 298-299; History of Chatham, by William C. Smith, pages 330-331.

The Narrow Land, by Elizabeth Reynard, pages 261-265; Pieces of Old Cape Cod, by Josephine Buck Ivanoff, pages 65-67.

Stories from Prohibition Days

Boston Globe, "Bodies Told Tale of Torture at Sea," by David Arnold, July 31, 1996.

Oh, For a Cot in the Wilderness

Shipmasters of Cape Cod, by Henry C. Kittredge, pages 206-220.

A Whale, a Tale & the 1893 Chicago Fair

Article from the Barnstable Patriot, August 2, 1892, "A Live Sperm Whale."

CHAPTER 4: SHIPWRECKS

The Girl Named for a Shipwreck

The Descendents of Robert Linnell, by Rachel Linnell Wynn, Gateway Press, Inc. Baltimore, MD, 1994, page 33.

Barnstable Patriot, Vol. XXVII, No. 33, February 3, 1857, page 3.

A History of Early Orleans, Ruth L. Barnard, Orleans Historical Society, Orleans, MA, 1975, page 97.

Wreck of the Steamer Portland

Shipwrecks on Cape Cod, by Isaac C. Small, pages 27-30; Cape Cod Annals, by Marise Fawsett, pages 89-97.

www.stellwagen.noaa.gov/maritime/portland

Dangerous Cargo

Pilgrim Returns to Cape Cod, by Edward Rowe Snow, pages 55-58.

The Blueberry Shipwreck

Cape Cod Standard Times, February 3, 1939; Barnstable Patriot, February 9, 1939.

Shipwrecks Around Cape Cod, by Bill Quinn. Lower Cape Publishing, Orleans, MA. page 139.

CG 36500 & the Pendleton

Chatham: The Lifeboatmen, by Bernard C. Webber, "Rescue CG 36500" pamphlet by Orleans Historical Society (Text by John A. Ullman).

CHAPTER 5: LIGHTHOUSES

Women Lighthouse Keepers

Lighthouses of Cape Cod, Martha's Vineyard, and Nantucket: Their History and Lore, Admont G. Clark, Parnassus Imprints, East Orleans, MA, 1992, pages 33, 34, 80, and 95.

Women Who Kept the Lights: An Illustrated History of Female Lighthouse Keepers, Mary Louise Clifford and J. Candace Clifford, Cypress Communications, Williamsburg, VA, 1993, pages 106 and 160.

History of Barnstable County, Simeon L. Deyo, 1890, pages 556 and 793.

USLSS to the Rescue

When Cape Cod Men Saved Lives, by Edward Janes; The Lifesavers of Cape Cod, by J.W. Dalton, pages 5-57.

"The Lifesavers of Cape Cod" pamphlet by National Park Service (Text: Mike Whatley)

The Monomoy Disaster

The Lifesavers of Cape Cod by Dalton, pages 122-125, 132-141; A Pilgrim Returns to Cape Cod by Edward Rowe Snow, pages 367-368,

Cape Cod Pilot by Jeremiah Digges (Josef Berger) pages 289-291.

CHAPTER 6: INDEPENDENCE

A Flame of Fire

Genealogical Notes of Barnstable Families, by Amos Otis, pages 222-224; Barnstable – Three Centuries of a Cape Cod Town, by Donald G. Trayser, pages 186-195; The History of Cape Cod – Vol. I, by Frederick Freeman, pages 398-399, 445, 545-547.

Quarrel & Conflict

Barnstable – Three Centuries of a Cape Cod Town, by Donald G. Trayser, pages 124-125; The Narrow Land, by Elizabeth Reynard, pages 186-190.

On Independency, Barnstable Voted No!

History of Cape Cod, Frederick Freeman, Volume II, pages 309-313.

Cape Cod: Its People and Their History, Henry C. Kittredge, pages 126 -127.

Two Unsung Revolutionary Heroes

King Sears: Politician and Protest in a Decade of Revolution, by Robert J. Christen. Arno Press, New York, NY. 1968

Enoch Crosby, Secret Agent of the Neutral Ground: His Own Story, by James H. Pickering, Published in New York History, Vol. WLVII, No. 1, January 1966, pages 61-73.

CHAPTER 7: AT WAR

The War of 1812

A Ruinous and Unhappy War: New England and the War of 1812, by James H. Ellis. Algora Publishers, New York, New York, 2009.

New England and the Sea, by Robert Albion, William Baker and Benjamin Labaree, Wesleyan University Press, Middletown, CN, 1972.

Cape Cod: Its People and Their History, by Henry C. Kittredge, Houghton Mifflin Co., Boston, MA. 1968, pages 134 – 144.

1812 Tricksters

Cape Cod Pilot, by Jeremiah Digges (Joseph Berger), pages 155-156, 181-182; A History of Early Orleans, by Ruth L. Barnard, page 67.

Cape Cod Legends by Elizabeth Shoemaker, The Berkeley Press, Boston, MA, 1935, page 27.

Cape Cod and the War of the Rebellion

Cape Cod Times, "His Branded Hand was Abolitionists' Call to Arms," by James Coogan, January 16, 1983.

U-boat Attack

Cape Cod Pilot, by Jeremiah Digges (Joseph berger), pages 130-132; A History of Early Orleans, by Ruth L. Barnard, pages 150-154.

Cape Cod's Way, by Scott Corbett, pages 253-254; New York Times, July 21, 1918.

CHAPTER 8: LOST AND FOUND

Died with the Smallpox

History of Chatham, by William C. Smith, pages 325-328, 384.

Truro's Tower of Love
My Pamet by Tom Kane, 1989; page 252.

A Cape Codder's Gift to Japan
Interview with Sebastian Dotson, spring of 2013 (expert on Japanese photography and Renjo Shimooka.) Several references to Wilson in Barnstable. See Barnstable Patriot May 14, 1917

Marconi Cape Cod & the Titanic
Cape Codder, "Marconi Ignited the Spark of Global Communication," by Carol Dumas, January 10, 2003.

"Marconi and his South Wellfleet Wireless," pamphlet by National Park Servive (Text by Glen Kaye & Mike Whatley)

A Night to Remember, by Walter Lord. Bantam Books, New York, NY, 1997, page 51.

Titanic – Destination Disaster, by Eaton, John P. and Charles A. Haas. WW Norton, New York, NY, 1996.

www.qsl.net/g3yrc/Titanic.htm

Helen Keller's Cape Cod Connection
Helen Keller: A Life, by Dorothy Herrmann. Alfred A. Knopf, New York, 1998.

The Story of My Life, edited by John Macy, 1903

Helen and Teacher: The Story of Helen Keller and Annie Sullivan Macy, by Joseph Lash, Delacorte Press, 1980.

Barnstable Patriot: January 23, 1860, January 25, 1881, June 19, 1883, July 29, 1884, January 11, 1887, June 3, 1890, July 6, 1896, September 14, 1896, September 13, 1897, June 29, 1903, October 10, 1904, October 5, 1908, July 7, 1913, December 24, 1917

CHAPTER 9: DARK SECRETS

The Witch of Halfway Pond
The Narrow Land, by Elizabeth Reynard, pages 167-175; Genealogical Notes of Barnstable Familes by Amos Otis, pages 99-103.

Witchcraft in Old and New England by George L. Kittredge, Harvard University Press, Cambridge, MA, 1929, pages 20-21.

The Caper, "Dateline: Cape Cod," by Evelyn Lawson, October 19, 1978.

Love Gone Wrong
The Narrow Land, by Eliabeth Reynard, pages 41-44, 50-52, 208-217; Of Plymouth Plantation 1620-1647 by William Bradford, pages 189-192.

Cape Cod: Its People and Their History, by Henry C. Kittredge, pages 216-219; Cape Cod Pilot, by Jeremiah Digges (Joseph Berger) pages 193-197.

The White Witch
A Pilgrim Returns to Cape Cod, by Edward Rowe Snow, pages 237-239; Barnstable: Three Centuries by Donald G. Trayser, pages 277-282.

Shipmasters of Cape Cod, by Henry C. Kittredge, pages 111-120; www.factmonster.com (Fox Sisters)

Eugene O'Neill's Revenge on a Provincetown Librarian
Eugene O'Neill: Beyond Mourning and Tragedy, by Stephen A. Black, Yale University Press, New Haven, Conn. 1999.

Provincetown as a Stage, by Leona Rust Egan, Parnassus Imprints, Orleans, MA. 1994. Pages 232 – 239.

The authors wish to recognize the contributions of all the various libraries, museums, historical societies, and archives across Cape Cod that provided much valuable information toward the research and writing of this book, including: Barnstable Vital records; Mashpee Archives/Vital Records; Old Dartmouth Historical Society; Pilgrim Hall Museum; Sandwich Historical Society; Sturgis Library, Brooks Library, and the William Brewster Nickerson Room at Cape Cod Community College.

ACKNOWLEDGMENTS

Over the years I've had the good fortune to connect with many people who, like me, had an interest in Cape Cod history. Many of them were associated with historical societies, libraries and archives and they were generous in giving me access to a wide range of material. I owe them a great debt. And as I am quick to tell people, I was always an historian but it was my partner Jack Sheedy who made me a writer. I value his friendship and counsel very much. I should also acknowledge the support of my family. My children, who are now grown, undoubtedly remember lots of vacation trips to historical sites when I'm sure they would have preferred visiting amusement parks. I thank them for humoring me and indulging me in my passion for history. Finally, nothing can ever be accomplished without the encouragement and understanding of a loving partner. My wife Beth put herself second on many occasions where history in one form or another took me away from things that I should have been doing around the house. Hers was a special support that I very much appreciate. It made my efforts in this collection of essays possible.

Jim Coogan

Once again, with this book I wish to recognize the many Cape libraries, historical societies, and museums that provided assistance to me over the past thirty years of research and writing on this and previous books. These are invaluable institutions of knowledge and learning that warrant the continued support of the communities they serve. As always, I thank my family and friends who have always been in my corner – particularly my wife, Adriana, and our now grown children, Melissa and Gregory, who were infants when I first embarked on this Cape Cod history trek a quarter century ago. My sincere gratitude goes to my writing companion, co-author, and "older brother" Jim Coogan who has made this journey so enjoyable over the past twenty years. Writers tend to be a solitary lot – tapping away in the quiet of their room – but to have a co-author on five books is quite an accomplishment. And lastly, I wish to once again acknowledge those folks from centuries ago who created the marvelous history that warrants our continued remembrance.

Jack Sheedy

A SPECIAL THANK YOU

A special thank you to our book designer, Kristen vonHentschel, not only for her work on this book, but also for her work on three of our previous books: *Cape Cod Companion, Cape Cod Voyage,* and *Cape Odd*. We've been fortunate over the years to have had her professional expertise and easy-going personality in working on these books. Putting a book together from scratch is no easy business, especially when you have two authors involved. But Kristen has always made the process a smooth one, and for that, and for *Cape Cod Collected,* we are grateful.

Jim & Jack

The painting, "Highland Light," on the cover of this book is by Sandwich artist Kathryn Kleekamp.

The authors wish to thank Kathryn for the use of her painting. Her work is known nationally and her paintings are highly sought after. We feel privileged to be able to use an example of Kathryn's work in *Cape Cod Collected.*

Readers may visit her website at www.SandwichArt.com

Jim & Jack

ABOUT THE AUTHORS

Jim Coogan is a well-known Cape Cod historian. An award-winning author (*Sail Away Ladies: Stories of Cape Cod Women in the Age of Sail**), he is a frequent lecturer and commentator on topics related to the Cape. Raised in the town of Brewster in the birthplace home of Cape Cod novelist Joseph C. Lincoln, Jim was grounded at an early age in the wonderful history and lore of this famous peninsula. He has written twelve books filled with stories and tales about Cape Cod for children and adults. Retired after almost three decades as a high school history teacher, Jim is a former columnist for both the *Cape Cod Times* daily newspaper and the *Barnstable Patriot*. Since 1994 he has contributed to the *Barnstable Patriot's* Cape history publication *Summerscape*.** This is his fifth collaboration with Dennis author Jack Sheedy. Jim lives in Sandwich with his wife Beth.

Jack Sheedy is the author of seven books and of more than 800 published articles and essays. His books include *Cape Odd* and *Cape Cod Harvest****, both written with Jim Coogan, and *Dennis Journal*, which he co-published with the Dennis Historical Society. Publishing his first article at age 23, for the past ten years Jack has written a blog on the Cape Cod Today website. Since 1989 he has served on the writing team of the *Barnstable Patriot's* history supplement, *Summerscape* – five times awarded first place for editorial excellence by the New England Newspaper & Press Association**. Jack has written copy for a number of organizations, including the John F. Kennedy Library in Boston and the Arts Foundation of Cape Cod. He has appeared on HGTV and NPR radio speaking about Cape Cod history and lore. Jack and his family live in Dennis.

* *United States Maritime Literature Award "Best Book" – 2004*
** *First place for editorial content – weekly newspaper/editorial supplement – 1995, 1999, 2008, 2013 & 2014*
*** *Finalist in the "History: United States" category in the National Best Books 2007 Awards*

Back cover photo by Adriana Sheedy, taken "some years ago" at Sesuit Harbor in Dennis. The harbor was the location of the 19th century Shiverick Shipyards, which built eight clipper ships between 1849 and 1863.

Made in United States
Orlando, FL
22 July 2023

35363584R00080